COME
AND go

COME AND go

LIVING ON MISSION WITH GOD

ESTHER TERRY

Come and Go: Living on Mission with God

Copyright © 2020 by Esther Terry

All Scripture quotations, unless otherwise noted, are taken from the New International Version®, (1984). Grand Rapids: Zondervan Publishing House. Used by permission. On some occasions, Bible verses have been paraphrased and are not intended as an exact rendering of recognized translations; these passages are not enclosed in quotation marks.

Note: In some stories, the names have been changed to protect anonymity.

Cover design by Jerod Terry

Interior formatting by Tall Pine Books | tallpinebooks.com
and Blue Lake Design | *bluelakedesign.com*

Editing by Kari Lee | *kari.lee.editing@gmail.com*

This edition: ISBN 978-1-7338558-0-8 (paperback)

Printed in the United States of America

"As the Father has sent me, I am sending you."

JESUS (JOHN 20:21)

CONTENTS

DEDICATION &
ACKNOWLEDGMENTS

This book is dedicated to my mom, Willy Maasbach. I will always remember your love and faithfulness to Jesus and your family. You have lived the life of powerful prayer before me all my life. And to my father, the late Johan Maasbach, whose consistent example of passion to seek and save the lost has greatly impacted my life. I thank God for their obedience to follow Jesus and show me the meaning of living on mission with God.

I also want to thank:

My husband, Jerry. You are my best friend and partner in ministry and you continue to faithfully support me to walk in my God-given calling.

My children, Jaime and Steve, Rachelle and Ruben, and Jerod and Tara, for your encouragement along the way and for allowing me to use your stories. You have made a significant contribution to this book.

Special appreciation to Jaime and Rachelle for your great insights and commitment to help communicate my heart more effectively. Jerod, for using your creative gift to design the front cover of this book. Lori Zaleski for assisting me in developing the discussion questions and Kellee Krause for your initial editing. I appreciate your dedication and patience during this process.

My church family, Calvary's Love, whom we are privileged to serve. You have the heart of Christ to be His hands and feet in this world of darkness. Thank you for allowing me to use your personal stories, showing what it looks like to live on mission with God.

My praying family and friends, who have interceded before the throne of grace for me and this project. Thank you for standing in faith and prayer with me.

All honor and glory to my precious Savior, the Lord Jesus Christ, for laying down Your life for the salvation of mankind. You are my greatest example of what it means to COME to the Father and GO, living on mission with Him. May every reader know You and make You known!

TO MY CHILDREN'S CHILDREN:

Caleb, Aliyah, Elijah, Joshua, Grace, Honor, Iuliana, and Ezra:

My deepest desire and fervent prayer is that you will love Jesus with all your heart, soul, mind, and strength; be faithful to proclaim the Gospel of our Lord Jesus Christ; and make disciples of all nations.

> "We will tell the next generation the praiseworthy deeds of the Lord, His power, and the wonders He has done...so the next generation would know them, even the children yet to be born, and they in turn would tell their children." (Psalm 78:4-6)

1

THE HEART

As I climbed into my hygienist's chair so she could begin my dental check-up, I asked about her holidays. "It was a very tough time," Liz responded. Concerned, I inquired what made her Christmas so difficult. She confided in me that her husband had left her after twenty-four years of marriage. I could sense her sorrow and was heartbroken for her. While she was working on my teeth, she told me of her pain and the struggle concerning her two children.

"Liz," I responded, "You need Jesus. You can't do this alone and He wants to help you in your pain. I've just been reading about how Jesus is the Good Shepherd who promised to never leave us or forsake us." She told me she had just started going to church and I promised to send her an encouraging book about Jesus the Shepherd with the prayer that it would comfort and bring her closer to Him.

Six months later, I was back at the dentist office and saw Liz again. It seemed she was carrying the weight of the world. I asked how she was doing, to which she responded, "I'm trying to hang in there."

"Are you turning to the Lord with your heavy feelings?" I gently asked. I knew she had gone back to her church and was reading the Bible. "I feel distant from God, and He doesn't seem to answer my prayer," she replied. I asked her if she had ever made a conscious decision to receive Christ into her life, and if she had a personal relationship with Jesus. She said she could not remember if she had ever made such a decision but was sure she did not have a personal relationship with Jesus.

I was praying for Liz while she was working on my teeth. How I wished I could just have a normal conversation with her, instead of getting a few sentences in between rinses. Thankfully, there was frequent rinsing! I told her I would love to call her, so I could explain how she could have a personal relationship with Jesus. Then the Holy Spirit whispered these words to me: "Ask if she can take a short break after this appointment to talk to her in person." I hesitated since I had never done this before. Then I simply asked, "Can you take a short break after this appointment, so I can explain it to you?" She told me she had an hour lunch break right after my appointment and gratefully accepted my invitation.

We went to the park, which was right around the corner, and there on a picnic bench, I shared with her how God had truly heard her prayer by putting me in her path. I never go to the dentist in the middle of the day, and I 'happened' to be scheduled right before her lunch break. This showed her how personal and amazing God is. I walked her through the gospel message about a relationship with Christ. Liz sincerely repented of her sin and prayed with me on that park bench as she put her faith in Jesus as her Savior. She was a bit stuck on the thought that she needed to prove to God that she would trust Him by doing certain things. I simply explained that there was absolutely nothing she needed to do to prove herself. He had done everything already for her. The miracle happened. She now understood the gospel message and how it applied to her. God made a way for us to connect and she received the message of salvation. Liz now attends a life-giving church near her home where she is nurtured in her new life in Christ.

As an extreme introvert and timid teenager, I was the least likely person to share my faith. Though my father, the late Johan Maasbach, was a bold evangelist and pastor, I struggled with shyness and fear. At youth retreats, our leaders rallied us to reach our friends for Christ and I left with my stomach in knots. I greatly desired other people to know Christ and knew I should share about Him, but questioned how I could do so when I lacked the courage to even talk to people I knew. I loved Jesus, but was afraid and at a loss for what to say.

It baffles me that God would choose this shy introvert to share the gospel with so many people. He has graciously given me opportunities to lead others to Christ and granted me His heart for them. I find encouragement in the knowledge that God uses all types of people to share about Him in countless ways. God has not reserved this privilege for just the outgoing and bold personalities, but for *every* believer. It is His heart that compels me. "Go into all the world and preach the gospel to all creation" (Mark 16:15). He paid for this gospel with His blood, the cross paving the way for all to know Him.

At eight years old, I went to our mission church office to "work for Jesus" every Wednesday afternoon and help with different projects. Children in The Netherlands are free from school at that time. Usually I arrived during the afternoon staff prayer meeting. I remember sitting in the middle of the room, listening to the prayers of everyone around me as they all raised their voices together in one accord. These workers were crying out to God with all their hearts for the lost to be saved. Though we had religious freedom where I grew up in The Netherlands, I recall how often they interceded for the Iron Curtain—which separated Eastern Europe from Western Europe for forty-five years after World War II—to fall and for the liberty to worship Christ to be restored. We supported those who went behind the Iron Curtain to bring Bibles to our persecuted brothers and sisters in Eastern Europe and beyond, knowing only God could bring freedom. These powerful times of prayer made an impact on my young heart. Years later in 1989 when the news broke that the Iron Curtain had fallen, my mind went back to the fervent prayer meetings that I had been part of as a young child. Now churches and missionaries minister freely, their light shining unhindered by the laws of men.

My father was always an example to me, and I am grateful for the legacy he left behind. He never pressured me: "Esther, you really need to witness!" Instead, he inspired me with his example. He looked for every possible means to reach the greatest number of people. My father was pioneering churches in The Netherlands, reaching people at home and in other nations through a world-wide mission's ministry, but he was also reaching out to those he encountered in his personal life on a daily basis.

As I waited for him to finish at the checkout counter, he would be chatting with the cashier about life and then take the opportunity to tell of God's love for every person. Before he turned to leave, he would always leave the gospel behind in the form of a booklet. My father planted a seed in my heart to look for opportunities to share my faith and to share it all the time. He never went anywhere without taking plenty of resources to share the love of Jesus so that he could be prepared in every situation. He also involved our family in reaching out to people. One such memory is imprinted on my mind from when I was a young teenager. On the last day of our family camping vacation, he gave my brothers, sisters, and I a stack of printed gospel stories and sent the older kids to hand them out to the families who were on vacation from many different European countries. I remember walking from tent to tent feeling reluctant because I was painfully shy.

Following our canvasing of the campground, all six of us children followed my father's instruction to stand in a group at the campground entrance as he led us in singing songs about Jesus for the campers. My parents were such an example of this that it was normal for us. It was the culture of our family and this definitely left a lasting impression on me. My father consistently exemplified the heart of our heavenly Father who came to seek that which was lost. This produced fruit in all his children and grandchildren, who are each involved in building God's kingdom today. I am not emphasizing particular methods we used to share the gospel many years ago, but rather, that I grew up watching a lifestyle of sharing the good news at every opportunity. Methods change, but the message remains the same. As I grew to know Jesus more for myself, His heart began to compel me beyond my own limitations.

Sadly, recent surveys reveal that only two percent of believers share their faith regularly; 95 percent have never led a person to Christ. How can we change this staggering statistic in the church?

"What must I do to inherit eternal life?" an intrigued lawyer asked Jesus in the book of Luke (Luke 10:25-37, NKJV). I imagine Jesus did not hesitate when He responded, "What is written in the law? So he answered: "You shall love the Lord your God with all your heart, with all your soul, with all your strength, and with all your mind, and 'your neighbor as yourself.'" Jesus said to him, "You have answered rightly; do this and you will live." In this, the Savior was showing the close connection between loving God and loving others. In fact, the call to love God *is* a call to love others. "And who is my neighbor?" the lawyer pressed.

> The call to love God is a call to love others.

In response to this, Jesus described the example of a most unlikely witness. Probably to the man's surprise, Jesus' parable highlighted the compassionate effort of one Samaritan man to serve the needs of a dying Jew. The fact that this foreigner, whose race the Jews despised and whose journey and resource had another purpose, stopped and served, proves something of significance… his *heart*.

He did not stop because he was indebted to the victim, or because he had a medical degree. Certainly no one would have imagined someone like him would stop for this Jewish man. He simply had a heart of compassion and made himself *available.* It is easy to love those who love us, or those who think and act in the same ways as us.

Jesus says, "If you love those who love you, what reward will you get? Are not even the tax collectors doing that? And if you greet only your brothers, what are you doing more than others? Do not even pagans do that?" (Matthew 5:46-47). God loves every person and He tells us to love our neighbor with *His* love. He promised to pour out *His* abundant love into our hearts by the Holy Spirit, whom He has given us (Romans 5:5). His love never runs out!

Two Jewish religious leaders both happened upon the same man yet chose to pass him by. If the Samaritan would not have had a heart of compassion for this man, he would have continued his journey in the same way. But, as he arrived on the dreadful scene of a man beaten and alone, he took pity on him and with great compassion, "kneeling beside him, the Samaritan soothed his wounds with medicine and bandaged them. Then he put the man on his donkey and walked along beside him till they came to an inn, where he nursed him through the night" (Luke 10:31-34, LB). The Samaritan also paid for all the man's expenses (Luke 10:35).

Jesus said the priest and the Levite came down that road *'by chance'*; however, it does not say the Samaritan traveled in the same way. He journeyed with a destiny. It was intended that he traveled this road. In the same way, Christ-followers are not here by chance, but are marked with divine purpose and are called to fulfill it!

Without the compassion of this Samaritan, the man would have died. God desires to give us *His* heart of love and compassion for others. We must never reduce compassion to a mere feeling. It is a feeling that provokes *action*. God's call is to love with a heart of His compassion and make disciples. Who is suffering around you? Some we may recognize quickly as a person in need, but others may appear to have life neatly together. Regardless, a soul without a true relationship with Jesus is a soul that is suffering. God calls us to go where they are, even to those who are within church walls yet do not know Him. We must bring them to the "inn," the place of restoration and care in Christ. *This* is loving God.

This lawyer who approached Jesus knew that to inherit life, he had to love God and love his neighbor as himself. As a Jewish man, he was acquainted with this central command in the law of his people. But Jesus added in essence, you know it, but if you *do* these things, you will live. How then can we receive God's heart for those without Christ, those who are aimlessly on their way to eternal damnation?

In this story, the Good Samaritan is a picture of Jesus Christ who came to rescue us from death, offering abundant life. He too was perceived by many as the 'unlikely' person to be the Savior of the world. "Can anything good come out of Nazareth?" (John 1:46 NKJV). God the Father had chosen Jesus as the Appointed One to demonstrate His love by purchasing our salvation. Just as the Good Samaritan seemed to be an unlikely choice to reach out, we may also feel like we fit that description. But regardless of your own self-doubt or hesitation, rejoice and rest assured that God has appointed you! I was that unlikely person and I never felt qualified or brave enough to share the gospel. To this day, I do not feel capable in my own strength, yet He has showed me that by His grace, I am chosen and appointed to share His love to a lost and dying world through the power of His Spirit! "You did not choose me, but I chose you and appointed you to go and bear fruit – fruit that will last" (John 15:16).

It makes me also think of the scripture, "He chose...the things that are NOT – to nullify the things that are, so that no one may boast before Him" (1 Corinthians 1:28-29). I have the word "not" circled in my Bible, because it includes everything: not strong enough, not brave enough, not good enough, not gifted enough, simply, not enough! The Bible is filled with 'unlikely' people whom God used to show His glory. Through the years, God has been forming His heart in me and He continues to do so. What God has done for me, He can do for anyone. Developing His heart is an ongoing process, but "The One who calls you is faithful, and He will do it" (1 Thessalonians 5:24).

1. Accept the Invitation.

"Come, follow me...and I will make you (to become) fishers of men" (Matthew 4:19). To understand and accept this invitation to come follow Him has transformed my life. What a privilege to answer His call to follow Him daily. Remember these two words, "come" and "go." God intended our passion for reaching others to be motivated by our personal relationship with Him. He desires to fill us each day with more of Himself. Once we taste of His goodness and experience His presence, we will want more of Him. If we do not *come* to Him, we may not experience the desire, the compassion, or the strength to *go* and reach others.

When Jesus called, "Come, follow me," He was not merely enlisting some fishermen for service. He was calling them to *Himself*. God is not just interested in what we can do *for* Him, but rather what we will do *with* Him and *through* Him. He calls us to come, a divine invitation to relationship with Him.

Jesus also said, '*Come to me* all you who are weary and burdened and I will give you rest'" (Matthew 11:28).

He knows that we get weary and do not have what it takes to accomplish His will, but as we continue to come to Him in true communion, we will abide in His rest. He called us to come and follow Him and promised to make us "fishers of men." Being a "fisher of men," or an active personal witness for Jesus, is the act of "going." Clearly, He revealed we cannot *go for* Him without *coming to* Him first; yet, we also cannot come to Him and simply stay.

> We cannot go for Him without coming to Him first; yet, we also cannot come to Him and simply stay.

These two ideas work together. Simply put, when we come, we will also go, and when we go, we must continue to come.

2. Obey the Great Commission of Christ.

As believers, we share the gospel of Jesus because He commanded us to do so. This is His plan. Hudson Taylor stated, "The great commission is not an option to be considered. It is a command to be obeyed."

Before ascending into Heaven, Jesus looked into the faces of those He loved and commanded, "All authority in heaven and on earth has been given to me. Therefore, go and make disciples of all nations, baptizing them in the name of the Father and of the Son and of the Holy Spirit and teaching them to obey everything, I have commanded you. And surely, I am with you always, to the very end of the age" (Matthew 28:18-20). Later He added, "But you shall receive power when the Holy Spirit comes on you. And you shall be my witnesses in Jerusalem, and in Judea and Samaria and to the ends of the earth" (Acts 1:8). With His commission branded on their hearts, they personally went in the power of His Spirit and did just that.

Terry, a man on our missions team, was dreading the thought of flyering and ministering at a kids' outreach. He felt anxious and wasn't sure what to expect. Though we prepared the team and prayed together, he was afraid of taking this step until he obeyed and just did it! As he went, he became bolder in reaching out to the families and was completely set free of any fear and doubt. Instead of dread, he was filled with joy. Since then, Terry has gone on another missions trip and actually looked forward to being involved in *any* kind of outreach. This new freedom has also enabled him to reach out to people at church and in his own community. Terry says in his own words: "Each time I step out of my comfort zone, my confidence grows. I have experienced the truth of this statement: 'God doesn't call the equipped. He equips the called.'"

Jesus left His church the greatest story ever told to pass on to all. I do not always "feel like sharing," and many times opportunities do not come at a convenient time, but I do it out of love and

> The One who knows how to reach every individual, every culture, and every generation is with us and working through us by the power of His Spirit.

obedience to God. In obeying His command, we must remember, as scripture says, that He has all authority. We share Jesus through Him who has all power and authority and He has promised He will always be with us. The One who knows how to reach every individual, every culture, and every generation is with us and working through us by the power of His Spirit. "Then the disciples went out and preached everywhere, and the Lord worked with them and confirmed His word by the signs that accompanied it" (Mark 16:20).

I sometimes hear people are waiting to share Christ until they have a "heart for it" or feel "gifted" to share. I have found simply obeying the Great Commission produces His heart in me. In other words, as I obey His heart, He conforms my heart to His.

3. Renew Your Love Relationship with God.

What makes a person go out of his or her way to become a personal witness for Christ? What motivates missionaries to sacrifice the comfort of home and family for another country in order to share the gospel? Even our greatest human motivation will never endure like the love of our Almighty God.

We all share a deep need for God's supernatural love in our hearts. The Father loves us deeply and desires to reveal His love to us. I had one such encounter as a young adult. I was praying for God to show His love to me. I kept praying, "God, please show me your love." As if it happened yesterday, I remember opening my Bible and seeing Romans 5:8, "But God demonstrates His own love for us in this: While we were still sinners, Christ died for us." Though this is a basic truth that I had heard all my life, it became personal revelation in that moment. My heart was overwhelmed by this experience of God's love. He showed Himself to me and I have never forgotten the truth this encounter taught me.

Whether we feel God's love at the moment or not, He has forever demonstrated it on the cross. God showed me His love is not based on my performance, what I do or don't do, but it is based on what HE has done! "But when the kindness and love of God our Savior appeared, He saved us, not because of righteous things we had done, but because of His mercy… so that, having been justified by His grace, we might become heirs having the hope of eternal life" (Titus 3:4-7).

Jesus prayed the world would know God loves us as much as He loves His only Son (John 17:23). This is just unbelievable and mindboggling! He loves us unconditionally. You may know this fact in your mind, but are you assured of it in your heart? He selflessly poured out His unconditional love to those around Him and laid down His life. It is this kind of love that compels us, and He invites us to do the same. "Greater love has no one than this, that he lay down his life for his friends" (John 15:13).

Paul declared, "For Christ's love *compels* us" (2 Corinthians 5:14). One of the hindrances believers face in freely sharing their faith is their own drift from God's love. How is your relationship with God? We still live in a time of grace where we have a God-given opportunity to grow closer to God and know Him intimately. "Not everyone who says to me, 'Lord, Lord,' will enter the kingdom of heaven, but only he who does the will of My Father who is in heaven" (Matthew 7:21).

With this warning, God alerted the church of Ephesus: "I know your deeds, your hard work and your perseverance...You have persevered and have endured hardships for My name and have not grown weary. Yet I hold this against you. You have forsaken your first love. Remember the height from which you have fallen. Repent and do the things you did at first. If you do not repent, I will come to you and remove your lamp-stand from its place" (Revelation 2:2-5).

When we cool off in our love relationship with Jesus, the light of our lives grows dim and no longer shines in contrast to a dark world. The answer? Draw near to Jesus with repentance and renew your relationship with Him. It's all about returning to Him! Yes, above all else, let's repent and return to His heart. The closer we are to Him, the true Light of the world, the more freely we will shine.

When my husband Jerry and I became lead pastors of Calvary's Love Church, we were extremely busy pioneering many new ministries. I loved being home with my children for many years as they were growing up. A new season had come as God directed me to assist my husband in pioneering this new church with many administrative responsibilities. During that time, it dawned on me that my heart seemed less passionate for the lost.

This realization devastated me, and I brought my heart before the Lord. God gave me the above verses and pointed out verse five: "Repent and do the things you did at first." He was showing me that the pioneering business of the church had distracted me from the opportunity to do personal evangelism. All I had to do was simply *do it again* and God would restore His passionate heart for the lost in me.

It is easy to drift away from His heart, while doing important, good things, even ministry. I obeyed what He had showed me, and through it, I felt restored in my heart. "Christ's love compels us" (2 Corinthians 5:14).

4. Understand the Fear of God.

Isn't it remarkable that Paul talks about Christ's love compelling us and yet, three verses earlier, he makes the statement, "Since then, we know what it is to fear the Lord, we try to persuade men" (2 Corinthians 5:11). As sinners we deserve eternal death, but God's love provides the way of redemption. God is just and righteous. "For the wages of sin is death, but the gift of God is eternal life in Christ Jesus our Lord" (Romans 6:23).

For this very reason, He gave His life as a ransom for many. It was the Father's love that sacrificed His Son on the cross. It remains man's free choice whether or not to receive God's gift of salvation, which determines his eternal destiny.

"For God did not send His Son into the world to condemn the world, but to save the world through Him. Whoever believes in Him is not condemned, but whoever does not believe stands condemned already, because he has not believed in the name of God's one and only Son" (John 3:17-18).

If we truly believe this gospel, we should be gripped with the urgency of the message. In the parable of the rich man and poor Lazarus, Jesus speaks clearly of *heaven* and *hell* (Luke 16:19-31). The poor man died and was carried by the angels to Abraham's side. The rich man also died and was buried.

> If we truly believe this gospel, we should be gripped with the urgency of the message.

Suffering from torment, he looked up and saw Abraham far away with Lazarus by his side. He begged for Lazarus to cool his tongue because of the agony he suffered. Abraham explained that no one could cross the great divide that lay between them. The rich man pleaded for Abraham to send Lazarus to warn his five brothers, so they would not end up in the same terrible place of torment. Abraham told the rich man that his brothers were given opportunity to listen to the godly men and women still living on earth. The destinies of both men were irreversible at death. The reality of heaven and hell gives eternal perspective. Seeing people in the *light of eternity* motivates my heart every time!

5. Consider the Example of Jesus and Others.

Over the years, in addition to my father, examples of those who lived as personal witnesses have inspired me. I have seen the fruits of their lives in those who now call Jesus, "Savior." Biographies of those who boldly share their faith despite great personal cost have always inspired and reminded me to be thankful for my freedom to share Christ. Studying the life and ministry of Jesus, we find our greatest example in Him. Let us determine to be an example to the next generation and to those we influence.

6. Experience His Joy.

Once we experience God's joy in sharing Him, we will be excited for the next opportunity to share Him again. Sharing Jesus brings great joy both to the person who receives the message, as well as to the one sharing. You just get hooked! I have personally experienced this joy many times. The Bible says the angels in heaven rejoice over one sinner who repents (Luke 15:7). It is amazing to me that God allows the one involved in the process of witnessing to experience a dose of this heavenly joy. Nothing compares to the joy we experience when we share the good news of Jesus.

7. Understand the Urgency of Our Time.

A number of years ago, I had a dream I was riding in a car with other Christians. They were laughing and joking with one another, yet outside, to my horror, the sky was darkening and fire was falling. Inside, I felt an overwhelming alarm that the world was coming to an end yet the Christians in the car with me were not aware of what was happening. I cried out, "We have to get out of the car!" but no one noticed me. "Stop!" I cried louder, yet they ignored my call and seemed oblivious to the noise outside. In despair I screamed, "The world is coming to an end! We must flee!" Finally, they heard me and stopped the car. We ran outside to find a place to hide, but found only streets with closed doors. There were people in these homes who did not know Jesus. I turned to my friends and screamed, "We must warn them!" I kept screaming, "We must warn them! We must warn them!" I awoke with the words still in my mouth. This dream made the imminent return of Jesus a more urgent reality to me, reminding me it is our responsibility to warn others and share the wonderful gospel of His love and grace; yet, our time is short, and we are running out of time.

> "For the Lord himself will come down from heaven with a loud command, with the voice of the archangel and with the trumpet call of God, and the dead in Christ will rise first. After that, we who are still alive and are left will be caught up together with them in the clouds to meet the Lord in the air. And so, we will be with the Lord forever…I tell you, on that night two people will be in one bed; one will be taken and the other left. Two women will be grinding grain together; one will be taken and the other left" (1 Thessalonians 4:16-17; Luke 17:34-36).

Christ's return will bring incredible joy to those of us who are ready, but great distress to those who are not.

"As long as it is day, we must do the work of Him who sent Me. Night is coming when no one can work" (John 9:4). "…Now is the time of God's favor, now is the day of salvation" (2 Corinthians 6:2). We will help speed up the day of His coming by sharing our faith, because Jesus claimed, "And this gospel of the kingdom will be preached in all the world as a witness to all the nations, and then the end will come" (Matthew 24:14, NKJV). All the prophecies which must be fulfilled before His return are completed. This indicates His imminent return.

Understanding the urgency of the time will also increase the passion of God in us to reach those who do not know Him and tell them about Jesus. The apostle Paul urges us: "...Walk carefully... making the very most of your time on earth, recognizing and taking advantage of each opportunity and using it with wisdom and diligence, because the days are filled with evil" (Ephesians 5:15-16, AMP).

"He is...not willing that any should perish but that all should come to repentance" (2 Peter 3:9, NKJV). God is looking for those who will carry His heart for the world He loves. And He is more than prepared to form His heart in those who are willing to receive it.

> God is looking for those who will carry His heart for the world He loves. And He is more than prepared to form His heart in those who are willing to receive it.

"The Spirit of Christ is the spirit of missions. The nearer we get to Him, the more intensely missionary we become" (Henry Martyn).

REFLECTION AND APPLICATION

1. What speaks to you from the story of the Good Samaritan? He was not on the road by chance, and neither are we! How does the idea that you are marked with a divine purpose and appointed by God embolden you to the thought of sharing your faith?

2. In what ways have you felt like the "least likely" person to share the gospel?

3. Has there been a person in your life that has been an inspiration to you in their ability to witness? What specifically stands out to you about their capacity to share the gospel?

4. Statistics tell us that only two percent (2%) of believers share the Good News. Can you identify something that has held you back from witnessing to others? Are you willing to let Jesus help you overcome this obstacle?

5. We are called to *come* unto Jesus, and we are called to *go* make disciples. Describe how the acts of "come and go" work intricately and intimately together.

6. In this teaching, seven different ways were outlined through which God forms His heart in us for the world He loves. Was there one way in particular that stood out to you, and if so, why?

7. After this teaching, what steps will you take this week to allow God to form His heart in you and make you a true fisher of men?

2

THE TREASURES

John and Pat were an elderly couple who used to live next door to us. We enjoyed getting to know them through occasional friendly conversation in the driveway or across the backyard. Because of their age, my husband Jerry helped them by plowing the heavy New York snow that blanketed our community every winter. A delicious homemade apple pie was always their way of saying "thanks!" One December, we brought them a plate of Christmas cookies and invited them to our church Christmas production. They heartily agreed and attended. To our surprise, they did not stop after Christmas, but continued coming, and sometime later joined our church's membership class. Jerry explained to them that in order to be a member of our church, one must first be a member of God's family. John and Pat were religious people who had heard the gospel on other occasions in our church, but never made a personal decision to follow Jesus. What a joy it was to welcome them into the family of God as they put their trust in Jesus as Savior!

Not long after that, their two sons and daughters-in-law followed their example, and all joined God's family. John and Pat were involved in our church for several years and, in time, their son Gary received God's call to nursing home ministry. God used him to encourage many elderly people and lead them to Christ. Their granddaughter, Kelly, who had also committed her life to Christ, attended a Christian university and responded to God's call upon her life. She and her husband Jesse serve in a ministry, translating the Bible into tribal languages through which many people in other nations are hearing the gospel. When you reach out to someone, you never know how God may use that person's future salvation to multiply, thirty, sixty, or a hundred-fold.

We thank God for helping us recognize those beautiful treasures living right next door!

One night, we noticed the lights of an ambulance flashing next door and we rushed to check on our precious friends. To our surprise, the paramedics were frantically working to resuscitate our friend Pat. I wiped away tears as I watched the sad scene unfold in front of me. Pat slipped into eternity that very night. Though it was difficult to let her go, we were thankful for our relationship with her and even more so for her personal relationship with Jesus!

Though we may initially share Jesus with *one* individual, God sees *entire* families, cities, and nations, and He longs for the gospel to come to *all*. Those who need Him are everywhere, in every neighborhood, workplace, school, and city. Some we know quite well, and others are strangers to us. Some are kind-hearted and open, while others are cold and distant. Yet God created them in His image and placed great value on their lives; enough to give His own life for them. God counts them as treasures and longs to bring them into His family.

> Those who need Him are everywhere, in every neighborhood, workplace, school, and city.

To begin, God simply asks us to notice them. Do you recognize the "treasures" He places in your path? Once you do, look for an opportunity to show or share God's love. Though there are many, begin with one. *See* the one in front of you.

The Bible is filled with treasures. At first glance, some may appear to be rough around the edges, but God sees them as a valued treasure. He wants us to see every person we encounter as He sees them. Zacchaeus was a man of short stature, dishonest character, and selfish greed. His wallet was full and his friends were few. Interestingly, Zacchaeus *wanted* to see Jesus. There are people we meet along the way who have this same desire.

Jesus found Zacchaeus in a tree. Do not limit the places God may show you a treasure waiting to be found. Jesus was simply passing through the town (Luke 19). Often, it is along our way, as we are "passing through," that God wants to reveal to us those who need Him. As we walk through the grocery store, the coffee shop, the work place… may our simple prayer be this: "Lord, help me see one of Your treasures today." The crowd was pressing in around Jesus, both the seekers and skeptics. Struggling to see, the notorious tax collector, Zacchaeus, scrambled up a tree for a better view of the Savior. Who would imagine that this man would seek Jesus?

"Jesus...looked up and saw him, and said to him, 'Zacchaeus, come down immediately. I must stay at your house today'" (Luke 19:5). Jesus looked up and *saw* him. Others ignored Zacchaeus, but Jesus noticed him. The Lord had many to reach and disciples to teach, but He *noticed* this one and *stopped* for him. That expression of kindness would forever change the life of this troubled man. Jesus simply showed interest and kindness to have dinner with him. It broke religious laws and cultural norms for a rabbi to have dinner with a sinner such as Zacchaeus. Crowds demanded an audience with Jesus and followed Him almost everywhere He went, yet Jesus was moved more by the condition of Zacchaeus' soul than winning the approval of others.

Zacchaeus was so moved by the fact that Jesus saw him and desired company with him, he immediately blurted, "Look, Lord! Here and now, I give half of my possessions to the poor..." (Luke 19:8). What was that, Zacchaeus? And he doesn't stop there. "If I have cheated anybody out of anything, I will pay back four times the amount" (Luke 19:8). This tax collector was suddenly willing to dig deep into his own pockets and repay his victims...with interest!

Jesus did not mention repentance, but the Holy Spirit was at work. The Holy Spirit is always at work, doing what we cannot to prepare and convict the hearts of those who need Him. Jesus boldly and lovingly responded, "Today salvation has come to this house, because this man, too, is a son of Abraham. For the Son of Man came to seek and to save what was lost" (Luke 19:9). A lost treasure... found. Jesus noticed this treasure, showed interest in him, and displayed kindness. On His busy way, He could have missed him entirely, but He did not. It was the very last time Jesus passed this way, since He was on His way to Jerusalem to lay down His life. You never know when it will be the last time you have an opportunity to share Christ. Is there a Zacchaeus on your path? A kind neighbor, a difficult boss, a dear friend or an acquaintance at the gym? Who do you pass along the way? How does God see them?

> You never know when it will be the last time you have an opportunity to share Christ.

As I was admiring a display of baked goods in the entrance of a grocery store, I noticed a woman coming out of the store with tears in her eyes. "Are you okay?" I gently asked. To my surprise, she told me her son had stolen money from her to buy drugs. I quickly introduced myself and offered to pray for her. Debbie began to weep and granted me permission to pray with her. At that moment, the Holy Spirit came, and God did a miracle by lifting, the weight of oppression and anxiety from her through prayer. I was happy to tell her I had just come from 'Live Free,' an addiction recovery ministry at our church. She told me she had just prayed while shopping, "God, do You even see me? If You do, please, show Yourself to me." God answered her cry for help. He saw this treasure and He allowed me to see her as He led me to stop at a store where I rarely do my shopping. I suddenly realized I had been delayed several times on my way to the store. God's timing was perfect. He goes out of His way to connect with a treasure hidden in darkness. As we parted ways, she promised to bring her son to 'Live Free' the following week. I was overwhelmed with thankfulness.

Many people are simply "along our way." They are those we encounter naturally in everyday life, with whom we can share the love of Jesus in one way or another. Yet, there are others who are "out of our way," and God is looking for those who are willing to go to them. Some find themselves in dark places of difficult life circumstances. It is not always comfortable to reach them and at times it can get quite challenging or even messy.

I never forgot a vision my father received from God in his early years of ministry. When he was praying, he saw a big dark mud puddle with people in it. There were men standing around the puddle wearing black shiny shoes who would not enter the puddle for fear of dirtying their shoes. God was showing my father that if he wanted to see people rescued and saved from sin, he must also be willing to go into muddy and messy places. Isn't that what Jesus did? He left the glories of heaven and came to this earth to deal with the "mess" of our sin so we could be forgiven and receive eternal life!

No one would have seen potential or treasure in Saul. This zealous young man with a personal agenda against Christ-followers launched his vicious attack against the church to imprison and destroy the believers. We find his story in Acts 9:1-19. I am sure Ananias was shocked when God told him to go to a specific house on a specific street and pray for this man who seemed impossible to reach. Saul was not a man along Ananias' way. God not only saw the potential for faith in Saul, He was preparing to make him the greatest witness to the Gentile world. God would actually make him an apostle who would lay down his life for that which he had once despised! The Lord instructed Ananias to go, pray, and to participate in a miracle of grace. The blind and bewildered Saul was receiving his spiritual sight.

This moment of decision for Ananias was crucial. "Lord... *him*?!" The disciple reminded God of the evils he knew of Saul and admitted he was terrified to obey. What Ananias did not know was that the salvation of Gentiles, kings, the demon-possessed, and the devoutly religious was in the making. He did not know the writings of Saul would serve as Scripture for centuries to come or that God was already working in the life of this impossible man. God was inviting Ananias to simply join Him in the miracle. Would you be willing to go? Are you willing to go out of your way to reach the "Sauls" in your world even if God asked you to go into a dark or difficult place? They could be a former neighbor, a friend you haven't seen in a long time, an unbelieving relative, someone who is missing from your church family, or even another nation.

First, Ananias heard and received the directive from God. If he had not heard, his story would have looked very different! It was certainly not easy to seek out the man who had been such a threat to the early church. God's perspective was altogether different and His vision much larger than Ananias could have imagined. We need His perspective to transform our own limited outlook.

God was also very specific in His leading. He sees each individual within the chaotic darkness of our world. He knows their names, where they live, and what they do. He sees *them*, and He sees *you*. When we are sensitive to the leading of the Spirit and willing to view others as He does, we will make room for the supernatural work of God.

Although God directs us specifically at times, His Word simply tells us to *go*. In other words, when we go out of our way to reach those who do not know Him, we are obeying His command. Thankfully, Ananias obeyed and went. He simply joined God in the work He was doing in Saul. Defying fear and every other obstacle, he walked out of his way, laid hands on God's chosen instrument, and prayed. God did the rest. "Something like scales fell from Saul's eyes…" (Acts 9:18). Saul could see in every sense of the word, and he was never the same again. Neither was the world.

I cannot end this chapter without telling you about Tomal, a hard-shelled, young boy who attended our outreach program at a local school. "Mom's Night Out" was a God-given idea for a broken part of our community where fatherless children fought for attention and overwhelmed mothers struggled to hold life together. Because of school restrictions, we were not able to speak about Jesus, but we used His Word to teach valuable life skills such as communication, healthy family relationships, and wise use of finances. We offered prayer to those who shared their problems with us and invited them to our church. Getting involved exposed us to the pain and overwhelming life circumstances these women faced. Yet God repeatedly made it clear from His Word that He desired to heal the brokenhearted and set the captives free. He desired to "give (them) a crown of beauty instead of ashes, the oil of joy instead of mourning and a garment of praise instead of a spirit of despair." He promised us *those* who were healed and set free would in turn become the ones to help rebuild ruined lives "and restore the places long devastated, for His glory" (Isaiah 61:1-4). We regularly prayed these specific scriptures over the families we were called to reach with tears and intercession. At first, we hardly saw any progress. It looked impossible as we reached out to these broken lives filled with anger, people who found it difficult to trust or receive God's love. Yet God saw Tomal, a treasure hidden in darkness. A few years after attending the program, he walked through the doors of our church with his family. At first, it was a challenge, and he seemed unresponsive to the kid's church leaders who reached out to him in love.

One memorable day, a speaker transparently exposed her past, her want of a father, and her encounter with an amazing God. "God is a Father who will never leave you because of the depth of His love. It doesn't change." And with that, she challenged them to move toward God, to let *Him* be their Father. God was working beyond what we could see and Tomal responded. He poured out his heart to God, and the loving Father lifted the weight from Tomal's shoulders. With tears streaming down his face, Tomal committed his life to Jesus. For several years now, he has been serving as a loved youth leader in our church and gives the Father's love to youth and children daily, working at the school he attended years ago.

Tomal's brother Jose and his mom Luz also committed their lives to Christ during that time. In Luz's own words, "Jesus saw me when I was completely broken. I thank Him for rescuing me and my family from great darkness. God enabled me to forgive those who had hurt me, and He healed me from anger, bitterness, and pain of my past.

My life is completely restored by the power of God! He also miraculously healed my body from two strokes." Luz and her family are the fulfillment of God's promise in Isaiah 61. God has given Luz a heart of compassion for women who are broken, and He uses her to minister to them. Luz also continues to believe wholeheartedly for all her children and grandchildren to surrender their lives to Jesus.

> "And I will give you treasures hidden in the darkness, secret riches, and you will know that I am doing this – I, the Lord ... who called you by name, when you didn't not know me. I am Jehovah, there is no other God. I will strengthen you and send you out to victory... and all the world from east to west will know there is no other God" (Isaiah 45:3-6, LB).

God is calling you and me to see the treasures, both those who are "along our way," and those who are "out of our way," that we may participate with Him to see them transformed.

"Defend the cause of the weak and the fatherless, maintain the rights of the poor and oppressed. Rescue the weak and needy; deliver them from the hand of the wicked" (Psalm 82:3-4).

God is calling you and me to see the treasures, both those who are "along our way," and those who are "out of our way," that we may participate with Him to see them transformed.

"Do you not say, Four months more and then the harvest? I tell you, open your eyes and look at the fields! They are ripe for harvest . . . so that the sower and the reaper may be glad together" (John 4:35-36).

REFLECTION AND APPLICATION

1. What speaks to you from the story of Zacchaeus? The Holy Spirit was already doing a work in Zacchaeus before Jesus even spoke to him. In what way does the idea that the Holy Spirit is going before you and preparing hearts help you to be bolder in witnessing?

2. Take a moment to reflect on those with whom you come in contact with every day. Is there a treasure God is asking you to "see"?

3. Be creative! In what specific way can you connect with the treasure God has placed in your path and express His Love?

4. Often, God will ask us to notice people "along our way." Have you ever passed by someone and thought you should reach out and connect with them, but didn't? If so, what stopped you? What will you do differently the next time God places such an opportunity on your path?

5. Sometimes the treasures are "out of our way" and we must go to them. Does the idea of possibly going into a dark, uncomfortable place intimidate you? Are you willing to participate with God regardless of the fear? What do you think would have happened if Ananias had said "no" to God when he was asked to seek out Paul?

6. Has God ever given you a different perspective about someone that transformed the way you originally saw them? If so, how does this inspire you to seek a godly perspective toward other "treasures" God is asking you to reach?

7. After reading this chapter, what steps will you take this week to become sensitive to His leading to both see the treasures around you, "along the way," as well as those who are "out of your way," and show God's kindness?

3

THE HESITATION

The book of Exodus opens much like this:

Israel: God's chosen people now slaves in Egypt.
God: The mighty Deliverer with a powerful plan.
Moses: God's chosen instrument to deliver Israel…
scared out of his mind.

The day I was getting ready to focus on this subject, I opened my Bible to the next chapter in my reading sequence. I found myself in Exodus 3 and 4, the exact account of God's call to Moses from the embers of a burning bush. Moses responded with reluctance and hesitation. His inability to express himself adequately and possibly the mistakes of his past cast their shadow on his confidence. He did not feel a worthy spokesman for God, or maybe he was overwhelmed by the severity of Israel's plight.

We all have our reasons for hesitation when it comes to sharing our faith. When people respond to the gospel with indifference or offense, we lose confidence or hope for change. God knows our hesitations and our limitations. Without denying either one, He calls us to be His witnesses, expecting our total dependency on Him.

Unworthiness

Convinced we are not "good enough" to witness or be an example for others, we hesitate to share the truth we know because we feel unworthy. When struggling with my unworthiness as a young adult, God reminded me I will never be "good enough." This is the essence of the gospel. None of us are good apart from Christ (Romans 7:18). Because of this, the only One who is truly good died for us to make us good in Him and fully accepted by the Father (Ephesians 1:6, NKJV).

To remain preoccupied with our unworthiness is to be self-focused, and this hinders our freedom from knowing who we are in Christ. Our attention must be on Christ who forgives and cleanses us from all unrighteousness (1 John 1:9). Our worth is in Christ *alone* (1 Corinthians 1:30). Satan is the father of lies, and when we believe his lies about who God is, what He has said, or who we are in Christ, we enter into bondage that keeps us from being powerful witnesses for Christ. Believe the truth of God's Word, who He is, and who He has called you to be in Christ. In doing so, you will be set free and empowered by the Holy Spirit to be His witness!

Moses questioned, "What if they do not believe me or listen to me and say, 'The Lord did not appear to you'...O Lord, I have never been eloquent, neither in the past nor since you have spoken to your servant, I am slow of speech and tongue" (Exodus 4:1, 10). Interestingly but not surprisingly, God chose a spokesman who felt he could not speak.

God is never hindered by our weakness. Rather, our inadequacies present an opportunity for dependency, not upon self but upon the Almighty. In fact, God is seeking someone *willing* to *depend* on Him.

The Lord responded to Moses, "Who gave man his mouth? Who makes him deaf or mute? Who gives him sight or makes him blind? Is it not I, the Lord? Now go; I will help you speak and will teach you what to say" (Exodus 4:11-12).

Still unconvinced, Moses pleaded, "O Lord, please send someone else to do it." Have you ever said that? God consented to send his brother Aaron to aid and promised His own presence and Word would not be absent. Through obedience, Moses became a courageous messenger of God. None of us are truly qualified, but it is God's call and His life in us that qualifies us to represent Him.

> None of us are truly qualified, but it is God's call and His life in us that qualifies us to represent Him.

Fear to Offend

Many have taught that our faith is a private matter. True tolerance, they claim, will produce harmony and peace. Yet what peace exists on the "road to destruction" without Christ? What harmony is found in deception? "... All have sinned and fall short of the glory of God" (Romans 3:23). This is in direct contrast to biblical truth that must shape our worldview and understanding of eternity.

In life, we encounter those who seemingly have their life together, those who are busy juggling demands, or those who are uncomfortable discussing religion. It is easy to feel we are disturbing them or that they will not be interested in our message. However, we must remember, beneath the surface of every individual is a soul that craves a Savior. They may not admit or even understand that reality, but God has created each individual with a need and desire for Himself. It is only in Him that this need is fulfilled. Naturally, the way we approach a loved one or familiar friend will differ from our interaction with a stranger. We will discuss several methods of approach in chapter five.

> Beneath the surface of every individual is a soul that craves a Savior.

If you feel hesitant to share your faith for fear you may offend someone, consider this thought: If someone were dying of a terminal disease and you knew the cure, would you withhold it from him or her? Would you fear disturbing or offending this person? Jesus is the ultimate cure for the disease of sin, hardly an offense when understanding God's perspective of eternity. Some are offended by the truth of the gospel or because they do not see their need to repent of sin. Overcome the fear of men by a greater fear for God who holds the power over our eternal destiny. Jesus said: "And do not fear those who kill the body but cannot kill the soul. But rather fear

Him who is able to destroy both soul and body in hell" (Matthew 10:28 NKJV). The scripture also says: "In the fear of the Lord there is strong confidence" (Proverbs 14:26 NKJV).

Years ago, I was involved in an outreach in our community sharing about Jesus and inviting people to our church. At first, I felt concerned because I did not want to offend or bother any of the people we met. We were using a gentle approach. Eventually, we met an angry man embittered over the death of his wife. We were filled with compassion for him. He raged and we listened.

When he was finished "letting us have it," he stormed off, leaving us with heavy hearts. As I walked away, God clarified the situation for me. "Esther, feel more sorry for his soul dying in hell than for his flesh that is inconvenienced for a moment." This one statement removed my fear of offending others and shaped my perspective when sharing the gospel with people.

> Feel more sorry for his soul dying in hell than for his flesh that is inconvenienced for a moment.

Fear of Rejection

At times, we hesitate to start a conversation about Christ because we fear rejection. Because of our fear, we often falsely assume we will be rejected, when in reality, we may be pleasantly surprised by the openness and interest of people. Other times, we fear because the person seems unlikely to respond with faith. Concerning the "treasures" around us, we have already acknowledged even the unlikely can become transformed disciples of Christ. How did *you* make a commitment to Christ? Not everyone responds to truth the first time they hear it.

Linda joined God's family. She reminisced about a college friend who shared Jesus and a Bible with her. At the time, Linda did not show much interest. A year later, she visited our church and someone invited her to our New Beginnings group where we discuss the basics of our faith with new believers or those who are searching. We discussed the need of salvation with her, but she did not feel ready. Five weeks later, she made a commitment to Christ kneeling alone on her bedroom floor. The friend who gave her the Bible could have felt rejected, but this "seed" helped bring Linda closer to salvation. Ultimately, Linda did not reject the truth.

While working in an elementary school, my daughter Rachelle noticed Carrie, a single mom working as a custodian, trying to make ends meet. She befriended this woman, showing her kindness in various ways. Over time, she took the opportunity to speak to Carrie about Jesus and His great love for her. To Rachelle's disappointment, Carrie never responded with faith. This left Rachelle feeling her friend had rejected the message. *Ten* years later, this same custodian called Rachelle and joyfully recounted her decision to follow Christ, as well as her new involvement in her local church. My daughter was astounded first of all at her friend's decision to become a follower of Christ and at the grace of God that allowed her to find out about the answer to her prayers! A seed of the gospel can flourish long after it has been planted.

Let's say it takes seven seeds before one responds in faith to God. Maybe you were the first one to sow a seed, or the second, or third. Are those seeds sown in vain? Does an initial rejection mean a final decision? No, and so we continue to pray, to sow, and to trust God for growth. We are not always the one to reap the harvest, but often a part of the

> A seed of the gospel can flourish long after it has been planted.

process. Jesus said, "Thus the saying, 'One sows and another reaps' is true. I send you to reap what you have not worked for. Others have done the hard work, and you have reaped the benefits of their labor" (John 4:37-38).

As you speak about Jesus, you will from time to time encounter resistance or rejection. God is looking for those who are willing to live and speak the truth of the gospel. Jesus said: "If anyone is ashamed of me and my words in this adulterous and sinful generation, the Son of Man will be ashamed of them when he comes in his Father's glory with the holy angels" (Mark 8:38). We also must be sensitive to the Holy Spirit to not go further than what the person is ready for. In other words, know when to stop talking. You may need to end the conversation, encouraging him or her to think about what you have said.

Jesus entered Nazareth, eager to speak truth in the place of His childhood. However, they did not receive Him. We read they were "offended" with Him and, "He did not do many miracles there because of their lack of faith" (Matthew 13:54-58). Though many offensively rejected the Son of God and His message, He did not abandon His mission.

Sometimes people will reject our message, and in recognizing this, we identify with Jesus. It is not easy, comfortable, or enjoyable. Neither was the ridicule or judgment Jesus had to bear. He told us just as He was rejected so would we also be rejected because, in essence, those who reject the message we bring are actually rejecting Him.

Every year, Christians worldwide face growing persecution. Though there are believers who have swayed under the pressure of persecution, yet there are *many* who continue to share their faith. Why? Because they love Jesus and His love compels them to see people saved from eternal damnation. They have committed to obey the great commission. They share His heart and are determined to live like Him, "not willing that any should perish but that all should come to repentance" (2 Peter 3:9, NKJV). They understand their citizenship is in heaven (Philippians 3:20), and not on this earth. They will not love their lives, even unto death, for the sake of the gospel.

In our part of the world, we are abundantly blessed to freely share our faith. As time goes on, we may wonder how long we will have this incredible privilege. However, rejection, division or persecution in one form or another is inevitable at times for those who obey to be His witness and live a godly life in Christ Jesus (Luke 12:51-53). Paul said, "Yes, everyone who wants to live a godly life in Christ Jesus will be persecuted" (2 Timothy 3:12).

When we are committed to Jesus, speak the truth of the gospel, and refuse to conform to the culture around us, we might make those around us feel uncomfortable or even angry at times (Luke 4:28). As followers of Jesus, we must guard our heart against compromising God's message or principles in order to avoid criticism, opposition, or loss. God will enable us to endure patiently and stand strong as we abide in Jesus and hold firm to the truth of His Word. "For it is commendable if someone bears up under the pain of unjust suffering because he is conscious of God... If you suffer for doing good and endure it, this is commendable before God" (1 Peter 2:19, 20). "By standing firm, you will win your souls" (Luke 21:19, NLT).

Jesus was the most loving person who ever lived on the earth, yet He was ridiculed and rejected by many. Jesus said "Remember the words I spoke to you: 'No servant is greater than his master.' If they persecuted Me, they will persecute you also. If they obeyed My teaching, they will obey yours also. They will treat you this way because of my name, for they do not know the One who sent Me." (John 15:20-21). The scriptures remind us of the comforting truth that God always stands with those who endure suffering for His Kingdom's sake. "For He stands at the right hand of the needy one, to save his life from those who condemn him" (Psalm 109:31; see also Matthew 28:20, Acts 7:55, Hebrews 13:5b-6). God also promises the Spirit of His glory and eternal rewards.

> The scriptures remind us of the comforting truth that God always stands with those who endure suffering for His Kingdom's sake.

Fear of Failure

"What if they ask me a question and I don't know how to respond? What if I say the wrong thing?" The truth is, when we share Jesus, we are obeying His command, and that is always a win. Of course, it is our responsibility to present the gospel in a loving and graceful way, giving others opportunity to hear it. Yet God is responsible for the change in their heart. We are simply messengers of the greatest story ever told! When we've obeyed His command to share, we must leave the results to God. The apostle Paul said, "I planted, Apollos watered, but God gave the increase. So then neither he who plants is anything, nor he who waters, but God who gives the increase. Now he who plants and he who waters are one, and each will receive his own reward according to his own labor. For we are God's fellow workers…" (1 Corinthians 3:6-9, NKJV).

A person once told me, "Esther, I saw some of your flyers on the ground on Main Street yesterday. I could definitely tell you and your team had been there." I was disappointed. Had we failed? Should we not have gone to the city parade to meet those who gathered and hand them a simple flyer? Though this is definitely not the only way to share the gospel, I use this example to make a point. Upon receiving this news, I lifted my heart to God and immediately He reminded me of the parable of the sower.

"A farmer went out to sow his seed. As he was scattering the seed, some fell along the path, and the birds came and ate it up. Some fell on rocky places, where it did not have much soil. It sprang up quickly, because the soil was shallow. But when the sun came up, the plants were scorched, and they withered because they had no root. Other seed fell among the thorns, which grew up and choked the plants. Still other seed fell on good soil, where it produced a crop-a hundred, sixty or thirty times what was sown"(Matthew 13:3-9).

Jesus comforted my heart with this parable, and though this happened many years ago, I never forgot its message. He showed me though the farmer went out to sow, only one fourth of the seed fell on good ground, but it produced much fruit. The farmer had not failed because he did not reap a harvest of all the seed sown. He was simply obedient to sow the seed. "Along the path" represents the one who does not understand the Word, the hardened heart; the "rocky ground" represents the shallow heart, and "the thorns" represent the crowded heart (Matthew 13:18-23). There are many reasons why people may reject our message, however, whatever we do unto the Lord is never wasted.

Bill Bright stated, "Success in witnessing is simply taking the initiative to share Christ in the power of the Holy Spirit and leaving the results up to God."[1]

"Keep on sowing your seed, for you never know which will grow – perhaps it all will" (Ecclesiastes 11:6 TLB).

Personal Problems

We may hesitate because of our own personal problems. On the same day Jesus spoke of the parable of the sower, He experienced rejection and offense in His own hometown. He was also told about the brutal murder of his cousin, John the Baptist. Without a doubt, this was a difficult day for Jesus and His disciples. When Jesus heard these things, he left by boat to spent time with his disciples. However, the people followed him. "When Jesus … saw a large crowd, he had compassion on them and healed their sick" (Matthew 14:14). The entire day He ministered the Word of God and healed people.

The concerned disciples came to Jesus and said, "Jesus, send the crowds away so they can go to the villages and buy themselves some food" (Matthew 15). They saw the need and felt compassion, yet they were sure they were not the ones to meet the need. They felt they didn't have what it would take.

The crowd was overwhelming, yet Jesus challenged, "You give them something to eat"(Matthew 16). "What, me?" Andrew offered, "Here is a boy with five small   barley loaves and two small fish but how far will they go among so many?" (John 6:8). The truth of the matter was they did not have it within themselves to do anything for the people, but they gave what they had to Jesus. Taking the loaves and the fish, and looking up to heaven, Jesus showed His deep dependence upon His Father. Blessing it, He divided the fish among them all. They *received from Jesus* and started distributing the bread and fish, which seemed very insignificant. Jesus did not make the food only *enough*, He made it *more* than enough. Their baskets were overflowing. On the very day that they were dealing with the pain of offense, rejection, and loss, Jesus used the disciples to feed thousands of people. "They all ate and were satisfied, and the disciples picked up twelve basketfuls of broken pieces that were left over" (Matthew 14:20).

Sometimes we feel we have nothing to give because of stress or difficulty; yet, when we give ourselves to Jesus, we will receive from Him. *He* is always more than enough!

I have personally experienced this many times in my life. One day, I entered a store with a wounded heart; the burdens of my circumstances weighed heavily upon me. I prayed, "Jesus, strengthen me. Please send someone to strengthen me." I continued to pray under my breath, as a young cashier started helping me with my purchases. To my surprise, he began asking me all kinds of questions. Normally, I would have taken this as my cue to witness, but I just couldn't. I felt I had nothing to give, but he persisted. Finally, I inwardly said to the Lord, "okay, I get it. You want me to witness to this man." I began responding to his questions and told him how much Jesus loved him. We had a brief and fruitful conversation. As I exited the store, I realized my burdens were lifted. Rather than the heaviness of my situation, I felt rest and peace. God heard me and answered my prayer, even if it was in a different way than I expected. He truly had sent someone to strengthen me, a young man in need of a loving Savior. Do not let your personal problems keep you from reaching out to lost people. God may send them in your path as an answer to your prayer and strength for your personal needs!

"Pastor Esther, I want to introduce you to my friend Mary." These were Annie's words as I came to visit her in the hospital following a hip replacement. I realized she was still recovering from the surgery, but I also knew that this 84-year-old precious saint would not want to miss an opportunity to let her light shine. This was her passion. Annie asked me if I could pray with her friend Mary who seemed open to the Lord, and commented how she had some great conversations with Annie about God. I was not surprised when Annie told me she also needed more salvation booklets to hand out to nurses and doctors in the hospital because she had run out. I remembered her stories about how she would always take the opportunity to reach out to people. For years, she had done prison ministry, but now she was not able to leave her house because of physical challenges. This did not stop Annie. When a repair man or anyone else would come to her house, she would be sure to take the opportunity to tell them about Jesus, and with great joy tell us all about it! Annie did not let her age or her physical challenges stop her from living on mission with God. This was her joy and strength. As I left the hospital, I whispered in her ear that I felt Mary was ready to receive Christ... to which she nodded in agreement with a wink and a smile! I later found out Annie had led Mary to Christ!

Time Restraint

We can often miss an opportunity simply because we feel we cannot take the time for it. The next appointment, meeting, or personal commitment is always waiting for us.

James was picking up a couple of things before going out of town with his family for dinner. As he walked back to his car, he saw a man sitting on a bench just outside the store. James felt a nudge in his heart to stop and say hello to this man, but hesitated because he was already running late. He felt the nudge again, so he turned around to speak to the man. The man was surprised that James stopped to show genuine care. James ended up inviting Brian to church and assured the man he would give him a ride, if needed. To his pleasant surprise, Brian called to confirm the ride and also brought his friend, Andy. Both men were touched by God's presence and responded to the invitation to receive Christ. James and his wife, Brianne, came to the prayer room with the men, amazed and excited how God had used them. They told me the story about their time crunch and how thankful they were James stopped to talk to Brian despite his lack of time.

As a result of the unplanned delay, they changed their plans and went to a local restaurant instead. During dinner, their young daughter complained about an earache and was diagnosed with an ear infection at the walk-in clinic. James and Brianne were grateful they had not gone out of town. The simple decision to stop and greet this man not only led to the salvation of two people, but also ended up being in the best interest of their entire family. Since then, Brian and Andy have moved away, but we thank God for the connection they made.

In my experience, the Lord always seems to work out my schedule when I am obedient to respond to His opportunities. Though I have definitely also missed open doors to witness, I have never regretted the time I took to stop, listen, and connect with a person for the sake of the gospel.

Moses overcame his hesitation, feelings of inadequacy, and fear of rejection as he obeyed the Word of God by faith. "Now go, I will help you speak and will teach you what to say" (Exodus 4:12). As he went and obeyed, God was faithful to do what Moses could not.

How do we grow stronger in witnessing and overcome our hesitation? Step out in obedience and simply do it!

"Would that God would make hell so real to us that we cannot rest, heaven so real that we must have men there, Christ so real that our supreme motive and aim shall be to make the man of sorrow the man of joy by the conversion to Him of many" (Hudson Taylor).

REFLECTION AND APPLICATION

1. What speaks to you from the story of Moses in Exodus 3 and 4 and the story of Jesus feeding the multitude in Matthew 14 and John 6?

2. Have you ever felt unworthy, unqualified, or not good enough to be an example or witness for Christ? How do our inadequacies provide an opportunity for dependence on God?

3. In what way does the idea we need to feel more concern over a person's eternal soul than their momentary inconvenience change or shape your perspective on offending someone with the gospel?

4. What are some healthy ways to process rejection or resistance when witnessing to others?

5. Was there ever a time fear of failure stopped you from sharing your faith? In what way does the parable of the sower give you a fresh outlook on sharing Christ with others?

6. Describe a time when Jesus took what little you had to offer and turned it into something far more than you ever expected.

7. How can we keep our time constraints from being a hinderance to our witnessing efforts?

8. After this teaching, what steps will you take this week to overcome any hesitation you might have about sharing your faith?

4

THE PREPARATION

Wouldn't you agree the unexpected encounters Jesus had with people "along His way" were divine appointments of God? Most often, Jesus was on His way to something, but He stopped and talked to those He met, which often led to eternal salvation. Just think about it... on His way to Galilee, He met the Samaritan woman and spoke to her about living water. As Jesus started on His way, He met the rich, young ruler who wanted to know about eternal life. As He was passing through Jericho, He stopped for Zacchacus, a man no one wanted to see. As He was leaving Jericho, blind Bartimaeus cried out to be healed. Each time, He had the right word of encouragement, of power, of truth. How did He always seem to have the right response for these unexpected, divine appointments?

God is sending people into our lives on divine appointment. Will we be prepared to stop and reach them? In later chapters, we will discuss practical methods of sharing our faith and the message we are to share. Yet even understanding this does not adequately prepare us in our heart. Life can leave us drained or driven toward our next task, sometimes causing us to miss what God is orchestrating.

Peter encourages us with these words: "But in your hearts set apart Christ as Lord. Always be prepared to give an answer to everyone who asks you to give the reason for the hope that you have" (1 Peter 3:15). The key? Set apart Christ as Lord on a daily basis. Jesus' submission and unity with the Father is our prime example.

Intimacy with the Father

It is easy to think that Jesus' divine encounters happened because He was the Son of God. However, Jesus *chose* to seek His Father in prayer which *prepared* Him for what He was to say and do. Jesus longs for us to live in an intimate relationship with Him just as He lived in relationship with His Father. He has fully provided this for us through His death and resurrection. Just think, He longs for a personal, intimate relationship with us, in the same way He enjoyed relationship with His Father! Incredible!

> Jesus longs for a personal, intimate relationship with us, in the same way He enjoyed relationship with His Father.

He declared, "...I do nothing on my own but speak just what the Father has taught me" (John 8:28).

"The Son can do nothing by Himself, He can do only what He sees His Father doing, because whatever the Father does, the Son also does. For the Father loves the Son and shows him all He does" (John 5:19-20).

He "prepared Himself" through nurturing daily intimacy with His Father.

Jesus Chose Prayer as His Process

- As He was water baptized (Luke 3:21)
- As He often withdrew to pray (Mark 1:35, Luke 5:16)
- As He prayed all night (Luke 6:12)
- Before He chose His disciples (Luke 6:12-16)
- Before He asked the important question (Luke 9:18)
- Before He was changed before His disciples (Luke 9:28-29)
- Before He taught the Lord's prayer (Luke 11:1-4)
- Before He extended the invitation, "Come to Me..." (Matthew 11:28-30)
- Before He walked on the water (Matthew 14:23)
- Before the fish and the loaves were multiplied (Matthew 14:19)
- Before He raised Lazarus from the dead (John 11:41-42)
- Before He was crucified (Matthew 26:39-44)
- He taught the parable of boldness in prayer (Luke 11:5-8)
- He taught the parable of persevering prayer (Luke 18:1-8)
- He taught the parable about the heart in prayer (Luke 18:9-14)

These are only a few examples of the many that are mentioned in scripture. Jesus was dependent on His relationship with His Father, and it was *His* abundant life that flowed out to touch others.

Prayer not only prepares us, it also prepares the ones we are to meet. In prayer, we can ask God to open a door of opportunity as Paul did.

> Prayer not only prepares us, it also prepares the ones we are to meet.

"Devote yourselves to prayer, being watchful and thankful. And pray for us, too, that *God may open a door for our message,* so that we may proclaim the mystery of Christ, for which I am in chains. Pray that I may proclaim it clearly, as I should" (Colossians 4:2-4).

While writing this chapter, my daughter Jaime shared her personal experience with me. This is her story:

"One Sunday afternoon, I felt overwhelmed with inadequacy. That morning in our service, I heard a powerful, compelling message about sharing the gospel with those in front of us, in our very own community. I knew God was drawing me to obey Him in the great commission but, honestly, I felt like a failure in this area. I was currently working with a team to put together a women's brunch, and had purchased two extra tickets to give away to women who did not attend our church. For the previous three weeks, I had invited ten different women and they had all declined. I had already given up on bringing guests with me to the event when this timely message was spoken in our church.

"In desperation, I knelt in my closet at home and whispered a prayer before God with tears and surrender. 'Jesus, I want to share Your love with those who need You, but I'm not good at it. I have tried and failed each time. If You desire to do this through my life, please open the doors and open my eyes to see what to do.'

"The next day, I stopped into a clothing store to pick up a shirt for my daughter. I approached the manager and asked if she had a different size available. She helped me and then unexpectedly asked, 'So, what do you do for a living?'

"I opened my mouth to tell her that I stay home with my children and instead, found myself saying, 'I do volunteer work.' I had never responded to a question about myself in that way and had no idea where that thought even came from.

"The manager, Jill, surprisingly asked, 'What kind of volunteer work?

"'Well,' I explained, 'it is through my church. Currently, I'm working on putting together a women's brunch.'

"I still wasn't recognizing that the Lord was answering my prayer and swinging the door wide open for me to share with someone who was searching for truth. However, her next question got my attention when she asked, 'What's your women's brunch about?'

"I decided to go right to the heart of it and shared with her that our theme was 'Beautiful' and that God desires for each of us to know that He has created us beautifully in His image to know Him and know our worth. This resonated with her and she explained how she had just responded to a blog that morning concerning the true beauty of women. She explained her frustration about body image and beauty in society today. As I listened, I realized the song that was playing in the store was about girls realizing that they are beautiful. I pointed this out to her and with wide eyes she said, 'You could invite me to your event. I would come.'

"Now *I* was the one with wide eyes. I had simply asked God to open the door for me and He actually had a complete stranger initiate the entire conversation and invite herself to our church! I pulled out the ticket that I had been carrying in my purse the last three weeks. She took it and promised me that she would come.

Jill not only attended the brunch but returned the following year and attended the next brunch. Recently, she has been visiting our Sunday morning services with her husband and sons. I am so humbled that she is coming and receiving the truth of the gospel for the first time. I realize that the preparation took place, not through my strength, but through my broken surrender in a moment of great weakness on my closet floor. It is not our ability that does the work, but rather our willingness to say yes and allow the Holy Spirit to work through us.

> It is not our ability that does the work, but rather our willingness to say yes and allow the Holy Spirit to work through us.

"I cannot end this story without also letting you know that in the same week, God provided another open door for the second ticket I purchased in faith. A dear childhood friend contacted me in crisis, even though we had lost touch over the years. She was the one God saw and had in mind for the other open seat. I realize God is always at work; I simply need to join Him in what He is already doing."

Not only are we encouraged to pray for open doors to share Jesus as we come into the secret place each day, but it's also a powerful way to pray *while we are in conversation* with someone.

My husband and I were seated next to a young Romanian woman on a flight from Romania. We had been enjoying conversation along the way as Corina chatted about her family and the work she loved. Corina wanted to know about our lives, which led us to tell her about our family, our church, and the people we are called to serve. Though we had been connecting in a great way, suddenly Corina ended the conversation and was no longer interested. At first, I was surprised and wondered what had caused the sudden change. I started praying for her and concluded she was turned off somehow with religion and church and didn't want anything to do with it. I decided to give her space as Jerry and I talked and rested on the long flight. At dinner time, Corina put the book down she had been reading. I did not want to finish our time together this way, and it was obvious to me she had been hurt in her life. I did not know what to say so I silently prayed for an open door. "Lord, open the door. Open the door to show Your love to this beautiful woman." I kept praying this simple prayer.

As I prayed, these words came to me: "Ask her a question. Ask her about religion in Romania and how the church and religion in her country is perceived by her generation." It seemed the Holy Spirit was directing me.

Breaking the silence, I turned to Corina, "May I ask you a question?" I approached her the way the Holy Spirit had showed me, and she showed immediate interest to let me know how disappointed she was with the church in Romania. She shared how she had grown up in a very traditional religious church, was gravely disappointed by it all, and was definitely going about it differently than her parents. I listened to Corina tell her story of frustration with her church. Then I spoke to her about a personal relationship with Jesus that is so different than formal religion. God Himself had opened the door to reconnect. The door that had been completely closed opened wide for an amazing opportunity to share the gospel about Jesus. She listened with interest, as it was not what she expected to hear. We exchanged emails and God used the situation to plant a seed in her heart. I believe and pray the seed will flourish and bring forth fruit.

The prayer Paul asked the church to pray long ago is a powerful prayer, and God is faithful to answer this prayer for open doors to enable us to share the good news of Jesus. I have personally experienced God opening doors in multiple ways. Many times, it's not because of what we are saying, but because of what the person is saying or asking that leads to an open door.

Jesus was prepared, not only because He nurtured His relationship with His Father daily, but also because He turned to Him in His darkest hour. How can we live on mission with God and share the love of Jesus if we ourselves are drowning in the cares of life? In the midst of increasing spiritual darkness, God is personally inviting us to surrender our burdens and make an *exchange* with the Father:

our anxiety for His peace, our burdens for His rest, our desires for His perfect plans.

"Do not be anxious about anything, but in everything, by prayer and petition, with thanksgiving, present your requests to God. And the peace of God, which transcends all understanding, will guard your hearts and your minds in Christ Jesus" (Philippians 4:6-7).

"Come to Me, all you who are weary and burdened, and I will give you rest. Take My yoke upon you and learn from Me, for I am gentle and humble in heart and you will find rest in your souls. For My yoke is easy and My burden is light" (Matthew 11:28-30). What a wonderful invitation! He, the One who created the heavens and earth and holds all eternity, invites us to *"come"* to Him.

In the above verse of scripture, Jesus speaks about two kinds of burdens, "my" burden and "His" (the Lord's) burden. It's hard for me to take on the *Lord's* burden of intercession, searching for the lost, bringing back the missing, binding up the injured and strengthening the weak (Ezekiel 34:16) when I am already overwhelmed with the burdens

> God is personally inviting us to surrender our burdens and make an *exchange* with the Father: our anxiety for His peace, our burdens for His rest, our desires for His perfect plans.

of my *own* life. I used to think that the burdens of the Lord were not always light, until I came to understand they are only light when I *first* give them to Him. When yoked together with Jesus, we receive His heart and then *His* burdens become *our* burdens. Though we are not capable of bearing the weight God carries for a lost world, He looks for those who will share it with Him. It is an incredible privilege that He involves us in carrying the burdens of *His heart*. In other words, my burdens become His and His burdens become mine. In essence, God's Word says, "Cast *all* your cares on Him, because He cares for you" and "Cast your burden on the Lord, and He shall sustain you" (1 Peter 5:7, Psalm 55:22 NKJV).

God's Word often enables me to make the exchange with the Father and *leave* my burdens at the foot of the cross.

The people of that day were familiar with the idea of the yoke. Yokes were placed on the shoulders of oxen to carry a particular burden. Like two oxen yoked together sharing the load, we are yoked together with Jesus. As we release the weight of care and responsibility in prayer onto Him and walk in step with Him, He alleviates our burden as He does the heavy lifting, granting us rest and peace.

Being yoked with Jesus also gives us the opportunity to learn from Him and discover His gentleness and humility. Who wouldn't want to come to Him, receive His rest, and be yoked with such a wonderful Lord? No matter how dark this world is or how heavy our burdens seem, Jesus is the true refuge and rest for our souls.

Jesus Himself exemplified this in the darkness of Gethsemane. On His knees, He relinquished the burden of the cross before the Father in prayer. The unbearable agony of the cross made Him desperate to press in, to receive from His Father. Nothing else mattered. His focus was on God the Father alone! He offered prayers and petition with loud cries and tears and surrendered (Hebrews 5:7). In this exchange, He was strengthened for obedience. Amazingly, the strength He received in His Father's presence not only prepared Him to endure His mission, but also flowed out to everyone He encountered that night, and on the most difficult day of His life. In contrast to the breakthrough Jesus experienced, the disciples, overcome with sorrow, were sleeping while Jesus was praying. They loved Him but were too weary to pray. They did not sense the same desperation Jesus did.

Every one of us gets weary or distracted at times, or we do not know how to pray, or we leave the place of prayer before truly breaking through. Like the disciples, we can get distracted by the pressure of heavy burdens, a busy life, social media, or even good works. Jesus told His disciples, "Could you men not keep watch with me for one hour?" Knowing what was ahead, He specifically warned Peter and asked him, "Peter… Watch and pray so that you will not fall into temptation. The spirit is willing, but the body is weak" (Matthew 26:40-41). The good news is He desires to strengthen us in our moment of weakness by His Spirit. When you are feeling distracted or weak and you do not know how to pray, the Holy Spirit is ready to help you intercede; you need

> When you are feeling distracted or weak and you do not know how to pray, the Holy Spirit is ready to help you intercede.

only to ask Him! He is *always* ready! "In the same way, the Spirit helps us in our weakness. We do not know what we ought to pray for, but the Spirit Himself intercedes for us with groans that words cannot express. And He who searches our hearts knows the mind of the Spirit because the Spirit intercedes for the saints in accordance with God's will" (Romans 8:26-27).

Jesus was so focused on His Father and the purpose for which He came that there was no room for distractions. It also makes me think of the words of a song we used to sing: "Turn your eyes upon Jesus, look full in His wonderful face, and the things of the earth will grow strangely dim, in the light of His glory and grace."

Prayer may start as a discipline, but will become a great delight once you encounter His presence and the revelation of His Word. Experiencing God's presence and deliverance, the Psalmist exclaims: "Oh, taste and see that the Lord is good!" (Psalm 34:8, NKJV). Do not give up. Your breakthrough will come sooner or later. Any sacrifice cannot compare to the great rewards we receive by being in this secret place with Him! I also want to encourage moms and dads with young children. I remember being up often during the night with my babies and feeling too weary to pray in the early morning. I learned how to take my children with me into His presence. While feeding my baby, I would draw near to Him in worship and prayer, or sitting on the floor next to my son by the toy chest, I would pray out loud to the Lord. It may not have been my preferred way, but it worked; and, without realizing, I was planting a seed of intercession into my child's heart. I found that God is not hindered or displeased when we take our children into the secret place with us! He longs to connect with us throughout our day, in all that we are doing. In the same way we take our children into the secret place with us, we can look for opportunities to invite them along as we live on mission with God.

Note the significant difference in the way Jesus ministered on the day He was crucified and the way the disciples responded. When Peter was questioned about knowing Jesus, he denied Him three times. In a moment of weakness, he was not prepared to deal with the immense pressure, not ready to give an answer for the hope that was in his heart. We may find it difficult to understand that Peter, who had lived and walked with Jesus, would deny knowing Him; however, this challenges me to ask myself, "do *I* live *prepared* to give those around me an opportunity to hear what God has done in my life? Do they know what Jesus means to me and how much I love Him?" All of us can probably identify with Peter about witnessing opportunities that we missed or messed up. I can for sure! Peter's failure to speak about knowing Jesus did not cause God to give up on him. It reminds me of the importance to respond to Jesus' call to *watch* and *pray* with Him during this crucial hour, so I can be prepared and strengthened for what's ahead and be ready to give an answer to everyone who asks me about my hope in Jesus.

The moment Peter denied Jesus, the Lord *turned* and *looked* straight at him without saying a word. Then Peter remembered the word of the Lord: "Before the rooster crows, you will deny Me three times. So Peter went out and wept bitterly" (Luke 22:61-62, NKJV). Through this painful, humbling experience, Peter learned he could not depend on his own strength and wisdom, though he loved Jesus and was strongly devoted to Him. By God's grace, he was completely restored after the resurrection of Jesus. The one who shrunk back out of fear, denying His Lord, became a powerful messenger of the gospel on the day of Pentecost. He later penned these words: "But even if you should suffer for what is right, you are blessed. Do not fear what they fear; do not be frightened. But in your hearts set apart Christ as Lord. Always be prepared to give an answer…" (1 Peter 3:14-15). I am sure Peter never forgot Jesus' eyes of burning love and compassion (Luke 22:61).

You might think Jesus looks at *you* with eyes of disapproval or disappointment. Perhaps because you missed an opportunity, made a mistake, or because there are people in your life who have looked or spoken to you in that way. Maybe you look to God through *their* eyes or even the way you perceive yourself. As mentioned earlier, He yearns with fervent desire for intimate relationship with you (Luke 22:15) and looks upon you with tender love (Mark 10:21). You are accepted in Jesus Christ, the Beloved (Ephesians 1:6, NKJV). When you believe and know this in your heart, you come into His presence with boldness!

> He yearns with fervent desire for intimate relationship with you and looks upon you with tender love.

Recognize Jesus' preparedness. Jesus was prepared to respond to His accusers with calm confidence: "I am He" (John 18:5). He was not afraid to acknowledge who He was, even though He knew it would cost His life.

- Jesus was prepared to pray for His enemies in the midst of the blow of suffering. "Father, forgive them, for they do not know what they are doing" (Luke 23:34).

- Jesus was prepared to care for His family and friends while hanging on the cross. "When Jesus saw His mother there, and the disciple whom He loved standing nearby, He said to his mother, 'Dear woman, here is your son,' and to the disciple, 'Here is your mother.' From that time on, this disciple took her into his home" (John 19:26-27).

- While He died on the cross for the *world,* He saw and heard the *one* who was crucified next to Him and was prepared to lead him into His kingdom. "I tell you the truth, today you will be with me in paradise" (Luke 23:43). Not only did Jesus receive strength from His Father through prayer, but the opportunity to welcome the thief into His kingdom must have strengthened Him in the midst of His pain.

We know when we abide in Jesus and His Word, we will get to know Him more. His lovingkindness also leads us to repentance (Romans 2:4) and produces a deeper conviction of sin as well as truth. When we do not recognize our shortcomings, or the enemy's lies, we begin to hinder our own witness. It is hard to share about the goodness of the Lord when we are weighed down by our failures or Satan's deceptions. Jesus offers us forgiveness and cleansing for ALL our sins and failures and He exposes the lies of the enemy. When we truly *believe* and *receive* this gift of grace, we will walk in His freedom. This freedom literally compels us to represent Him and help others know Him for themselves. We are free to give after we freely receive from Christ.

Nothing compares to what Jesus has suffered, but He is our example in our hardships. "Consider Him who endured such opposition from sinful men, so that you will not grow weary and lose heart" (Hebrews 12:3).

"The biopsy results are positive for Hodgkin's disease, cancer of the lymph nodes." These words came to me as a shock when the doctor gave Jaime and I the results of some tests. I felt as if my world came to a screeching halt. As I walked out of his office, I lifted up my heart to the Lord. "What, Lord? My 22- year-old daughter was just diagnosed with cancer?" Immediately, the Lord met me right then and there. He responded with His gentle voice, "Perplexed, but not in despair." Without a doubt, this was God speaking to me. I concluded, God was saying, "I understand you are perplexed, but no reason to despair." This must mean everything is going to be okay. The word I received in that moment with Him defeated my fear and replaced it with peace. It prepared me for the challenging time ahead. The entire passage became a strength to our family: "We are hard-pressed on every side, but not crushed; perplexed, but not in despair; persecuted, but not abandoned; struck down, but not destroyed. We always carry around in our body the death of Jesus, so that the life of Jesus may also be revealed in our body" (2 Corinthians 4:8-10).

I was scheduled for a dentist appointment following this doctor's appointment. I had to explain to my dentist the reason for being a bit late and he wondered why I was so calm. I shared how God had directed me to a verse of scripture right after the diagnosis and how God's Word had given me peace. From then on, I was able to talk to my dentist about the entire process since he first heard about it. He was always interested to know how Jaime was doing and gladly accepted a recording of her testimony of healing a few years later. During this same time, we were pioneering a new church and it seemed as if we were in an intense war.

This situation with our church and daughter made our family desperate to continually receive from the Lord. We felt utterly dependent on His daily Word which miraculously sustained us and gave us specific direction. Paul said, "Everything ... was written to teach us, so that through endurance and the encouragement of the Scriptures we might have hope" (Romans 15:4). Seeking and worshipping the One who overcame brought us closer to Him and we knew He was carrying us. A few verses later Paul said, "May the God of hope fill you with all joy and peace as you trust in Him, so that you may overflow with hope by the power of the Holy Spirit" (vs. 13). We recognized the hope Jesus received flowed out to others, and He desires the same for us. Sometimes we were not even trying to reach out, we were simply pursuing the Lord to help us deal with various situations. In doing so, He was abundantly gracious to fill us with hope that at times overflowed to others. God gave us many breakthroughs in our church at that time, and by the grace of God, our church, Calvary's Love, now shines brightly as a lighthouse on a hill in our community.

God used Jaime's sickness as an opportunity to witness to doctors, nurses, and many who were terminally ill. The hospital, filled with patients and medical professionals, opened up an entire new world to us, not only for Jaime to receive chemotherapy, but for us to share the good news of the gospel.

The trying circumstances of our lives did not change our mission, but rather created an opportunity for it. Paul witnessed the same fact: "...what has happened to me has really served to advance the gospel. As a result, it has become clear throughout the whole palace guard and to everyone else that I am in chains for Christ" (Philippians 1:12-13).

When Jaime shared her testimony in our church of how God had brought her through this trying time, several nurses came to visit. God filled our hearts with joy and anticipation for this opportunity to reach those who didn't know the love of the Father. Through a time of great uncertainty and difficulty, God gave us open doors to reach the lost and the broken which filled our hearts with comfort and purpose. The extent of the opportunities was far beyond our expectation. Jaime was asked to speak to medical students about her experience and shared with them how God was her strength and peace. Her story was also published on the front page of our newspaper with the heading, "Cancer Survivor Leans on God: A Triumph of Faith." Through this article, radio stations broadcasted her story in several states. Jaime was interviewed for national television in The Netherlands and thousands heard the message of God's love and faithfulness! Nothing in our lives is wasted when we belong to Christ. Everything that takes place can be an opportunity to reveal God's heart to those who do not know Him and thereby impact eternity!

If we do not get strengthened in His presence, we will not be able to rise above our circumstances, nor will we be effective to the fullest measure God intended. Jesus always remained focused on His mission, strengthened by His Father.

Before the cross, He lived this way always. The agony of the cross did not change His mission but rather created an open door for it, not just for the man hanging next to Him but for *all* who believe in His name. This way of life was not only preserved for Jesus, but for you and I who remain in Him. God longs to reveal Himself through His people. His work is not dependent on our circumstances, but rather on our dependency of who He is. We are reminded in Ephesians 3:20 which states that His works are exceedingly abundantly above all that we ask or think!

I cannot end this chapter without mentioning the powerful example Jesus gives us in giving thanks and praise as He shared the Lord's supper with His disciples just before He laid down His life. He gives thanks for His broken body and His blood poured out for the salvation of many *before* Gethsemane and *before* the cross. Jesus

> Nothing in our lives is wasted when we belong to Christ. Everything that takes place can be an opportunity to reveal God's heart to those who do not know Him and thereby impact eternity!

taught me I can give thanks *before* I see a promise fulfilled and *before* I see my prayer answered. Jesus gave thanks in the face of injustice, betrayal, and the agony of the cross!

Jesus gave thanks looking ahead to be with His Father and with all those who endured loving Him and will join Him in the marriage supper of the lamb (Mark 14:22-26). Simply put, "Give thanks in all circumstances, for this is God's will for you in Christ Jesus" (1 Thessalonians 5:18). Praise is also a powerful pathway into His presence and prepares our heart to connect with Him!

Coming to Him never excludes *going* out to represent Him, but rather prepares the way for it! Through this process, we learn to meet our divine appointments with a response like Jesus, produced from a heart that has been with Him.

Practical preparation is important as well. Preparing the right approach and resources that clearly explain the gospel are easily accessible and will help to assist and equip you in sharing your faith. Opportunities will arise with those you will not see again, like a waitress in a restaurant, a cashier, or a person you meet while traveling. It may make an eternal impact to leave them with a resource that explains the good news of the gospel.

Calvary's Love Church, where my husband and I pastor, provides digital resources such as videos, pictures, sermons and music through our website, social media, YouTube, and church app.

We also provide printed resources such as invites, event promos, Bibles and reading materials that clearly articulate the gospel. We have discovered that people are impacted by other people's transformation stories. We are intentional about capturing these stories in written form and on video. These serve to reflect God's love and the power of the gospel at work in their lives. And long after we are gone, the stories will still speak to the next generation.

Recall the Good Samaritan of whom we talked about in chapter one. When he stopped to help the beaten man on the side of the road, he was prepared with oil and bandages, just what the hurting man needed. Let's live prepared spiritually and practically, so God can use us anytime, anywhere. LIVE READY!

"Walking with God down the avenues of prayer we acquire something of His likeness, and unconsciously we become witnesses of His beauty and His grace" (E.M. Bounds).

"As you develop intimacy with God, the supernatural becomes natural" (Oswald Chambers).

REFLECTION AND APPLICATION

1. What speaks to you most about Jesus' intimacy with the Father? How does the example of Jesus in this chapter inspire you?

2. What does "Living on Divine Appointment" mean to you? Have you ever had a divine appointment? How were you prepared for the encounter?

3. What do you do to set apart Christ as Lord on a daily basis? What could you do to deepen that daily intimacy?

4. We are prepared to be His witness through prayer, the Word, praise, and thanksgiving. In your own words, explain how each of these enables us to be effective witnesses.

5. Explain how a lack of daily intimacy with God will affect our ability to live for Christ.

6. What are some things you can do to "practically prepare" to share the gospel?

7. After this lesson, what steps will you take this week to prepare yourself to live on mission?

5

THE APPROACH

I first met Carmen while picking up my children from school. Friendship and trust developed over time as we got to know each other over lunch or chatting in the parking lot. As time went on, she began to see the source of what shaped our lives. When Carmen began confiding in me about the struggles she faced, I shared the truths with her that had so often encouraged me.

"When I don't know what to do," I told Carmen one day, "I pray to God straight from my heart. I tell Him exactly how I feel, and I know He hears me. That is because this is so much more than a religion I practice; it is a deep relationship with God. The promises in the Bible are my strength in times like these." Then I gave her verses relating to her situation and offered to pray with her. She was always willing and thankful to hear about the difference Jesus made in my life, and eventually she anticipated these prayer times together. Over the years, we also invited Carmen and her family to special church events, which they attended from time to time.

A few years ago, during one difficult period of their lives, Carmen's husband, Robert, called me in despair. In this moment of marital crisis, he was reaching out for hope, unsure of how to find it. Carmen had left him, and he was broken. Her own disappointments and hurts had made her feel this was the best solution. As I listened to Robert share his painful story, I felt heartbroken for my dear friends. I expressed my heartfelt concern and explained that he simply could not do this without Christ. God opened the door to share the gospel with Robert that day, showing him the hope that could be his through faith and a relationship with Jesus. He was ready in that moment to give everything to God, so we prayed together for his salvation. The evident change in Robert was significant and this became apparent to Carmen. He continued to pray and show God's love to his wife though they were separated. Over time, and by His grace, God restored their marriage.

There is much to be said about the various approaches we can use to share our faith. In Jesus' interaction with the young rich ruler who was not willing to surrender all, it says, "Jesus looked at him and loved him" (Mark 10:21). "It is the goodness of God that leads people to repentance" (Romans 2:4). "He is patient… not wanting anyone to perish…" (2 Peter 3:9). This is the heart of God for all men.

Once we have been transformed by the love of Jesus, we will want to share Him with others. His life more naturally flows out of us because we are aware of the grace that God extended to us.

After building trust and friendship with them, Carmen and Robert more readily received the message we wanted to share. As you consider the following approaches, keep in mind, it's about loving people. Even as we encounter strangers we will not see again, God expects us to carry the same heart into our witnessing conversations.

If we enter a conversation that we know will end when the next customer walks into the store or the plane reaches its destination, we may more quickly begin discussing Christ than if we were talking with a colleague at work whom we encounter daily. Yet, one can never be sure how long an opportunity will last. In this cold, dark world, genuine interest goes a long way, even in those brief conversations with those you may not see again. After you make a connection through genuine conversation, pray for an open door of opportunity to share the love of Jesus. We can also receive guidance and promptings from the Holy Spirit. When we wait for Him to open a door, we can simply join Him in what He is orchestrating.

Jesus exemplified this when approaching the Samaritan woman. Upon her arrival at the well where Jesus was resting and waiting for His disciples to return, He simply began talking to her about water, the very thing for which she had come to the well. In other words, He began where she was. His genuine interest surprised her and opened the door for more conversation. This one conversation led to her receiving Him as the Messiah who was to come and also led many in the city to believe in Jesus (John 4:4-42).

Paul followed this same example in Acts 17:16-23. When Paul came to Athens, he was greatly distressed to see the city was full of idols. Is your heart deeply moved for those who do not know God? Paul approached the people in the temple as well as those in the market place. I imagine it was quite overwhelming to experience the crowds and see the city full of idols. He may have thought,

> In those moments, I stop looking at the crowd and start looking for "the one in front of me," the one God may be enabling me to reach at that moment.

"Where do I begin and who do I approach?" Often, I am also overwhelmed by crowds of people, wondering who knows the Lord and how I can reach them. In those moments, I stop looking at the crowd and start looking for "the one in front of me," the one God may be enabling me to reach at that moment.

This is what Paul did. He could not connect with the entire city, but he approached those who *happened* to be in the market place at that moment (vs. 17). God also orchestrated an opportunity for him to speak with some men. His approach was remarkable: "... I see that in every way you are very religious..." Paul started where they were. He continued, "For as I walked around and looked carefully at your objects of worship, I even found an altar with this inscription: 'To an unknown God.' Now what you worship as something unknown I am going to proclaim to you..." (vs. 22-23). The Holy Spirit helped Paul to start where they were and helped him to share about the living God whom they did not know. Though not everyone believed and accepted the truth about Jesus, several did and joined him (vs. 34).

Invitational Approach

In the parable of Luke 14, Jesus introduces the invitational approach. In this parable, a certain man invited many guests and sent his servant to inform them the meal was ready. Then the excuses began. This is a clear example that not everyone we invite will respond favorably to the gospel. The message of this parable: continue to invite people.

"…Go out quickly into the streets and lanes of the city, and bring in here the poor and the maimed and the lame and the blind. And the servant said, 'Master, it is done as you commanded and still there is room.' Then the master said…'Go out into the highways and hedges and compel them to come in, that my house may be filled" (Luke 14:21-23, NKJV).

Diane was excited her friend Karen was coming to our Women's Brunch, a special annual outreach with our church. Karen had come several times before, but always left before the speaker shared her message. Recently, Karen had gone through a very difficult time because of an alcohol addiction and had lost her license. Diane promised to give her a ride and was excited that her friend would be able to hear the message for the first time. Karen committed her life to Jesus Christ that day. Another miracle was that our scheduled event speaker had to cancel at the last minute and God led us to another speaker who shared how God delivered her from an alcohol addiction. This was exactly what Karen needed to hear. God is amazing! I believe there are times God orchestrates an entire event, service, or situation for the sake of reaching one person. A couple of weeks later, Karen suffered a fatal accident that took her life. Though we were grieved by this tragedy, we were thankful that Karen had accepted the Women's Brunch invitation and, above all, that she had responded to God's invitation to come to Him.

Eighty percent of people who come to church are invited by someone they know. Many people have come to Christ because someone invited them. I call this "the power of personal invitation." Consider inviting someone to a service, a small group you are attending, or a get together with Christian friends.

> Many people have come to Christ because someone invited them. I call this "the power of personal invitation."

My husband, Jerry, and son-in-law, Steve, initiated a conversation with their waitress, Heather, at a local restaurant. Jerry told Heather that my daughter and I were out of town speaking for a women's retreat and that he is a pastor. Heather said she had a desire to attend church and that her friend, Stacy, another waitress in the same restaurant, was interested in coming, as well.

They were able to connect with Stacy before they left. We were blessed to see both girls in our church service that following Sunday, and when the invitation for salvation was given, Heather responded to receive the love of the Father. A simple invitation led to Heather's salvation! Doesn't this make you wonder how many people are waiting for someone to invite them to church? Remember the power of personal invitation! Take advantage of special days of the year such as holidays and times of celebration like a baby dedication or water baptism. These occasions can be a perfect opportunity to invite a friend or family member.

It is also important to introduce those you invite to other believers, helping them connect to the body of Christ. They can be impacted as they experience the evidence of God's life in real relationships. When they do, they will recognize something genuine and inviting, which will help them understand the love of the Father.

Even though I find many people genuinely interested, some are not ready, like my hairdresser, Cara. It was easy to build a relationship with her because she was a very sweet girl and did a good job on my hair. We got to know each other as she talked about her life and I shared about mine. Cara belonged to a traditional church, but it was evident that she was turned off with "religion" as she put it, the result of several disappointments she experienced with her church. As I listened to her talk, I would respond and explain the difference between formal religion and a personal relationship with Jesus.

Whenever the subject came up, she never responded, and the conversation did not go very far. I invited her to our Christmas production, but she was not able to make it. Before she moved away to get married a few years ago, I was able to give her a gift and I included some powerful true stories. I was thankful for our relationship but felt very sad she had not been interested to know more about Jesus. I prayed that the few seeds I was able to sow would bring forth fruit someday. We need to remind ourselves it is our responsibility to sow the seed and give people an opportunity to hear the gospel, yet it is up to each person how they respond to the message. I was encouraged to know that a seed can bear fruit long after it is planted.

Another way of inviting people is through what we call "flyering." Our church does this at various times during the year. Teams pass out invitations throughout the city to a community-focused church event, sharing them with those they meet and leaving them on doors. Sometimes we include the gospel in a door hanger, making it look like a gift, and other times we just use an invitation. Though we invite people in our community through social media and invitations are sent through the mail, as well, we like the opportunity flyering gives to connect with people personally.

LoriAnn had not been walking with the Lord for several years after her husband died in a car accident. With a wounded heart over child abuse and her husband's tragic death, she was looking for a church but didn't know where to go. About that time, our church was running a kid's zone at a large community event.

Our team went out flyering among the crowd and offered bottles of water to people attending the event. LoriAnn received the flyer and came to visit our church the following Sunday. She was overwhelmed by the presence of God and committed her life to Jesus that same morning. She felt God had answered her prayer to find a church. God is healing and restoring LoriAnn and her family. A simple invitation led to a life change for an *entire family*!

Response Approach[2]

I was traveling home from Ecuador with a missions team from our church. The man beside me had turned his back to me, making no opportunity for conversation. One of our team members sitting behind me was showing me pictures from his recent missions trip to Romania when suddenly the man next to me spun around and blurted, "What are you doing looking at pictures from Romania? I am from Romania!

What a set up! The Holy Spirit had clearly orchestrated this open door. We were on a flight within the United States, coming from Ecuador, looking at pictures of Romania, and I sat next to a Romanian! Only God could have arranged that! As I talked with him about my daughter who lives in Romania and our experiences there, it became an open door to tell this puzzled man that our encounter was from God. It was, in fact, God's way of showing him that He sees him and wants to reveal Himself to him. I was able to speak to this man about a personal relationship with Jesus and left him with a booklet that explained it well. I have often experienced divine appointments such as these to share Jesus. We can always believe and pray with expectancy for God to orchestrate the right situation.

> We can always believe and pray with expectancy for God to orchestrate the right situation.

In the response approach, simply listen to what people say and respond accordingly. Use the conversation subject or situation to begin talking about your faith in Jesus. If you miss the opportunity, return to the subject, if possible, by contacting the individual again.

Jesus witnessed about His Father to Nicodemus by simply responding to his questions. This religious leader had a desire to seek and find the truth. He recognized, "'You are a teacher who has come from God. For no one could perform the miraculous signs you are doing if God were not with him.' ... Jesus declared, 'I tell you the truth, no one can see the kingdom of God unless he is born again'" (John 3:1-3). Nicodemus recognized that God was with Jesus and asked Him about it. Jesus responded to his questions and was prepared with an answer. It was to this religious leader He declared the simple but powerful gospel: "For God so loved the world that He gave His one and only Son, that whoever believes in Him, shall not perish but have eternal life" (John 3:16). Though Jesus responded to Nicodemus with truth, it seemed it was a process for him, as it was for many of us. The account of Nicodemus doesn't tell us exactly what took place when he came seeking that night. However, we do know he argued for fair treatment of Jesus later on and he accompanied Joseph of Arimathea to ask Pilate for the body of Jesus to be buried, donating seventy-five pounds of spices. This took courage and suggests that Nicodemus was transformed by hearing the words of the Savior (John 7:50-51, 19:39-40). Others should be able to recognize that God is with us. As we live "ready," we will more likely have the right responses.

With the response approach, there is often opportunity to offer prayer. When someone shares a need, offer to "say a word of prayer" with him or her, believing God will answer. God delights to reveal Himself to a person who does not know Him. This approach is especially relevant in society today as many people feel over-whelmed or anxious by their circumstances and the world around them. Another appropriate time for the response approach is during crisis. Whether it is your neighbor dealing with the loss of a loved one or a friend facing a personal tragedy, it is an opportunity to point them toward a loving God.

Testimonial Approach

Jaime was challenged by her science professor in college concerning her faith. One day he threw a Bible across the room and it landed on her desk as he sarcastically stated, "Some students dropped this off in my office. They must think that I need it or something."

My daughter whispered a prayer in her heart, asking God for wisdom how to respond. She affectionately touched the Bible and gently replied, "That's a pretty powerful book to throw across the room." And then quietly continued with her work.

After this, Jaime began praying for her professor and believed God would do a work in his heart. Before Christmas, she gave him an encouraging testimony on CD with a small gift. This softened his heart and they built a mutual relationship of respect during the next semester that included conversations about the Bible. After graduation, Jaime felt drawn to visit her professor and give him a copy of her personal testimony that she had shared at church. Several months later, she returned one last time to drop off a book that she had stumbled across that correlated his field of study with the Bible. During that brief visit, her professor told her with tears in his eyes that he had prayed the salvation prayer that was included at the end of her testimony CD. He received the book with much gratitude and told her, "I realize now the Bible doesn't contradict science, but they work hand in hand."

Peter and John were amazed at Jesus' words and miracles. They were greatly impacted by His death and resurrection. The fact He desired an intimate relationship with them was mind-boggling. These disciples wanted to share the resurrected Christ with everyone and simply could not stop proclaiming the good news of Jesus wherever they went (Acts 5:42, 8:4). They said, "For we cannot help speaking about what we have seen and heard" (Acts 4:20). When you are in daily relationship with God, you cannot help but tell others of what Jesus is doing in your life.

Many people around you are searching for hope and encouragement. When God opens the door, tell them about answers to prayer, the difference Jesus is making in your life, and how you have been transformed by following Him. The story of your life may be one of pain or blessing, but regardless, it is a testimony of God's personal encounter with you. It can make a significant impact as you share it with others. In John 9:25, the man born blind exclaimed, "One thing I do know, I was blind but now I see." Though many were opposing Jesus, no one could deny the testimony of this miracle.

Do you need a new experience with God to inspire fresh enthusiasm to tell your story? Not only are our salvation stories powerful, but also our encounters in our relationship with Christ. They enable others to see how this relationship relates to daily life. Henry Blackaby wrote:

"Your responsibility will not be to convince others of the reality of God, but simply to bear witness to what your Lord has said and done for you. The change in your life will be your greatest testimony of your relationship to Christ. There is nothing more appealing or convincing to a watching world than to hear the testimony of someone who has just been with Jesus."[3]

The flight to Holland was packed. I was sitting beside a very large man who could not help but take up his seat and half of mine. Needless to say, it was a long and interesting flight! Though he did not initiate conversation, it did not take long to find out he was a professional football player for the Colts and that for him, football was life. I asked him various questions of interest and listened as he eagerly talked about his passion.

When he directed the conversation toward my life, it was also entirely natural for me to speak about my passion of following Jesus and the difference Christ has made in me. When our lives are centered on Christ, the natural outflow will be our testimony of what He means to us. As we talked, it was evident that he was not familiar with having a personal relationship with Jesus. From my half of my seat, I shared with this strong, passionate athlete. He listened, and seed was

> When our lives are centered on Christ, the natural outflow will be our testimony of what He means to us.

planted. You never know how God will lead another to water or harvest fruit in a life, but we can believe He will.

Kathie wrote her personal testimony of how God miraculously delivered her from drugs and alcohol. Through the years, she has shared her story in the form of a booklet with family, friends, neighbors, and strangers she met along the way. It became a way of life for Kathie that anyone she came in contact with would receive her testimony with a fresh baked loaf of bread. "And they overcame him by the blood of the Lamb and by the word of their testimony, and they did not love their lives to the death" (Revelation 12:11, NKJV).

For many years, every July, we held our Sunday evening services in the parking lot of our church. Our worship team set up outside and several people from our church were scheduled to share personal stories of what God had done in their lives. The church family brought their own lawn chairs and invited a friend. We grilled hamburgers or had ice cream sundaes and games for the kids, enjoying time together afterwards. These were special, powerful nights for the whole family as we celebrated and glorified the God of miracles. In order for a greater number of people to hear these miraculous, personal stories, we just recently included them in a series on Sunday mornings. Our young generation needs to know Jesus' power is still the same today! ". . .We will tell the next generation the praiseworthy deeds of the Lord, His power and His wonders He has done" (Psalm 78:4b).

Besides sharing your own testimony, you may also share the powerful stories of others. What has God done in the lives of those you know?

Jesus told the disciples of John, who was struggling with doubt, "*Go* and tell John the things you have seen and heard: the blind see, the lame walk, the lepers are cleansed, the deaf hear, the dead are raised, the poor have the gospel preached to them" (Luke 7:22, NKJV). Each story is the proof the waiting world needs to see.

Serving Approach

A simple act of kindness will make a larger impact than we may realize. As we serve people with the love of Jesus, we are the evidence that God cares. Maybe you have a colleague whose car breaks down. You may not be capable of fixing it, but you can offer a ride. A neighbor may be

> As we serve people with the love of Jesus, we are the evidence that God cares.

financially struggling or in need of a baby sitter. A simple meal or free babysitting for an evening communicates genuine care and concern. In this way, we meet them where they are, in their place of need.

The centurion in Luke 7:2-10 was known in his city for loving his nation. He used his resources to serve the people in his community and highly valued the people who worked for him (vs. 2-5). Imagine if every follower of Jesus and every Bible-believing church was known for loving and valuing the people in their sphere of influence. It is worth noting the leaders whom the centurion served told Jesus, "This man deserves to have you do this, because he loves our nation and has built our synagogue." The centurion *himself* said, "Lord, don't trouble yourself, for I do not deserve to have you come under my roof... but say the word, and my servant will be healed." Though this great leader had many people working for him and understood the authority of his own words (vs. 8), the centurion was known as a servant leader who loved and valued people. This allowed him to impact those around him and the city in which he lived.

Through Rachelle's friendly interactions with her neighbor, she discovered his family's financial struggle. Though he never asked her for anything, Rachelle began making his family a meal periodically. When she could help them in some way, she tried to do so. Over time, she built trust and friendship with the family. The more they conversed, the more she was able to share that she derived the greatest meaning of her life from knowing God in true relationship. Her neighbor could see that through her life; she did not just believe something, but this belief affected the way she lived. This spoke volumes to him, and he agreed to visit her church. Since then he has committed his life to Jesus, and he was baptized after completing the New Beginnings course offered to new believers. Serving her neighbor opened his heart to hear about the God who cares for him. The Apostle Paul worked to become all things to all men so that by all possible means he might save some (1 Corinthians 9:22). Sometimes we are not able to meet the need ourselves, but we can direct them to someone who can.

A few years ago, a horrific flood devastated our community. Most people were affected in one way or another and many lost their homes. Our church responded with help by cleaning out homes and preparing meals. It became a wide-open door to respond to this great need in our community by showing the love of Jesus in a tangible way. Along with giving practical help, we listened to the heartbreaking stories of victims and offered them the hope of an indestructible heavenly home as we shared about our faith in Christ.

On the day Jesus fed the 5,000 men, women, and children, He showed compassion, not only by His ministry of teaching and healing, but by providing for their physical need for food. This act of compassion and the miracles He performed led the people to recognize that Jesus had come from God (John 6:14).

For many years, our church has organized an annual park outreach called Fun Fest in a neighborhood in our city. It is an opportunity for our entire church to unite and serve, demonstrating the compassion of Christ to our community. I am incredibly thankful for the freedom we have, to boldly declare the gospel in the outdoors! Each summer, this park becomes a place of joy and salvation for God's glory. We fill the park with inflatables and carnival games for children, activities for youth such as a basketball tournament, free haircuts, and a center with community resources for health care, rehabilitation, and counseling. We also serve free lunch and groceries to everyone. As we serve them in these ways, we have many opportunities to talk about Christ with people. We do this in one-on-one conversations, but also through the message of "family shows" with music and drama that are part of the special day and through resources we give guests as they leave. Many people respond every year to the invitation to know Jesus personally and we have had some incredible encounters in conversation and prayer with people. We have found people are searching and want to know that someone cares. When they experience the love of God through the attitude of those serving them, it makes an impact on members of our church family as well. We also follow up with every person who receives Christ.

What started as a neighborhood party in the park twenty-one years ago has grown into a community-wide event. Some people come annually and, each time, a seed is planted. Since we are involved with other community services in our area, it helps us to be more connected with our city and build relationships in a caring and tangible way. Many are in God's family today and part of our church because of this.

Prayer Approach

Though prayer can be offered as a response to someone who shares a need, prayer can also be used as a way of approach. When my husband and I eat in restaurants, we often ask our waiter or waitress if he or she has a specific need we can pray for later that day. We usually find them willing to express a need, which on many occasions has enabled us to share the love of Jesus or to invite them to church. We also try to leave something with them by way of a personal story, invitation, or website reference. It always amazes me how some people are eager to share about their struggles and are even willing to open up to someone they have never met!

Just the other day, we met Evie, a waitress who was serving us lunch. She told us she had come to our community to rebuild a relationship with her estranged father. With tears in her eyes, she quietly confided in us, "But unfortunately, that is not going to happen." In the short time we had with her, we told her of our loving heavenly Father who desires a personal relationship with her and who would never leave her. She received the words of hope and comfort and promised to visit our church. We are praying for her.

When John arrived at the hospital to visit his friend, he overheard someone talking on his cell phone who appeared to be in distress. After the man finished his conversation, John, who happened to be nearby, asked the man if he needed prayer. Dave was surprised and told John his wife had a heart attack and needed surgery that week. After praying, Dave expressed gratitude and John went on his way to visit his friend.

Later that day, John ran into Dave again at the hospital and discovered that he lived about an hour away, so he asked if he would like to get a bite to eat. At dinner, Dave shared he had not been in church for twenty years because of the hypocrisy of certain church members. John listened and assured Dave there are also many godly people who attend churches and shared with him how his negative experiences do not reflect the true love of the Father. John encouraged him that God Himself had orchestrated for them to meet and restore his hope.

John was able to continue sharing the love of Christ with Dave by sitting with him and his daughter during his wife's surgery. Dave ended up attending a men's breakfast and a Sunday morning service at our church while his wife was recovering. John had no idea that a simple offer to pray would lead one man to find hope and get reconnected with God. This was essential timing as we recently found out that Dave's wife passed away. He is finding strength and comfort in Jesus and started attending church near his home.

We met Ashley as she served my friend Marcia and me at a local restaurant. After some interaction and conversation, we simply asked our young server if she had anything we could pray for later that day. She asked us to pray for her siblings, who were living with her dad in another state. Her parents had recently divorced, and she was planning to join her father soon to help him. Her worry was evident. We asked her if she was part of a church in the area and she explained that she had been many years ago. After much time had passed, she was trying to find the friendly pastor she remembered named Jerry Terry.

Ashley was amazed when I told her I am his wife! Moved by the surprise of finding the pastor she was looking for, she opened up about her life and concerns about her family. We prayed with her right then, tears streaming down her face. No one was in the restaurant the entire time we talked to her. She was leaving the area and we just had these few moments to notice this treasure whom God had already prepared. A couple of days later, my friend dropped off some things for her to take along as she moved away. God's perfect timing amazes me!

Resourcing Approach

Giving a book or sharing a website or other such resource that reflects the gospel is a simple but useful approach. At the right moment, we can give something appropriate to communicate the truth to someone. A particular book, song, or message that encourages or answers the questions someone is asking about God or faith can be transformational. The supply is almost endless, so make use of good resources!

My family prayed for my uncle Peter's salvation for many years, but my uncle's heart remained closed, or so it seemed. One day, someone gave him a book about the second coming of Christ while he was on vacation. God opened his spiritual eyes and uncle

Peter committed himself to Jesus for the first time in his life. Several months later, he was diagnosed with cancer, and soon after, he slipped into eternity to meet His Savior. We are forever grateful to the person who handed my uncle this book and we know we will see him in heaven someday!

On the flight back from a missions trip to Ecuador, I met Elena. We exchanged brief introductions and I found out she was an Ecuadorian medical doctor on her way to China for training. I was very interested to hear about her passion and work. She then asked me about our reason for coming to Ecuador. In the course of the conversation, I found out she had a formal religious background. God opened the door to share the good news of a personal relationship with Christ. Elena was very interested, and we exchanged emails. I offered her the booklet of 'Steps to Peace with God' by Billy Graham, which she gladly accepted. A couple of months later, I received an email from Elena, saying, "I read the booklet and did what it said!" She received Christ on her own. The resource continued to speak to Elena even after our departure. I was thrilled to hear the great news!

Always be prepared with resources to share with others. When finding a good resource, let others know about it so they can share it within their sphere of influence.

A gift opens the way for the giver.

Gift Giving Approach

Another effective approach is simply giving a gift. "A gift opens the way for the giver" (Proverbs 18:16). Generosity itself reflects the character of God, and just as with serving, giving is a tangible testimony of God's love. You can give resources as a gift, as well. An appropriate book or devotional for someone who is interested or searching, a marriage devotional for a couple who is getting married, or a promise book for a religious person make great gifts. Of course, a Bible or a meaningful personal gift are excellent choices, as well.

Every year before the Christmas season, our church chooses a resource that explains the gospel in a relevant way, and we give it away. We wrap it up or bag it with some chocolate or candy and an invitation to our Christmas services. We encourage our church to carry some of these gifts in their cars or purses so they can have them on hand. It is incredibly rewarding to see the faces of busy cashiers, gas station attendants, or waiters upon receiving such a simple gift. They are always pleasantly surprised. Christmas time is a season where the hearts of many are more open for God and we must seize the moment!

When we started our church, we were praying about ways to reach our community. A quick call to the mayor's office informed us of several needs, including the many families facing financial hardship in our town. God led us to prepare gift boxes filled with toys, gloves, and hats (we called "love gifts") for these families. We were thrilled, but not sure specifically where these families lived. We knew there were a couple apartment buildings close by with families in great need. We went knocking on doors to find homes with children and offer them a gift for Christmas. At the second building, we met a young girl who showed us all the apartments where children lived. God was leading the way as He always does.

We needed the names of many more children, so we contacted a local school. Upon meeting the school social worker, she started weeping. While wiping away her tears, she told us she had been asking God, "Where is the church to help meet the needs of these families?" She helped us get in contact with many families in need, so we could give them gifts, as well, and we organized a special evening to meet the families and present the gifts.

By a miracle of God, we received permission from the school to hold the "Love Gift Night" in the school building, and invited all the families. We were also allowed to include the gospel with the gifts and present a short program for all the kids and their families. Seeing the smiling faces of many children has definitely been a highlight for our church for many years.

Several years ago, we requested permission from the school to hold the annual Love Gift Night at our church, so we could present a stronger message of the gospel. This has produced great fruit. Not only have hundreds of children and their families had an opportunity to hear the gospel, but many have responded to receive Christ and several families are part of our church family today.

This is Jasmine's story:

"I was raised in the south Bronx. I grew up in poverty and I can remember many hungry nights. I had a happy childhood for the most part, until the day that I suffered abuse as a young girl. Shame and pain filled my heart and I felt dirty and unlovable. I felt like people could look at me and see the filth that I felt inside. At 15 years old, I gave my heart to Jesus, but I wasn't quite ready to give Him my life. I got pregnant at a young age and I learned quickly to push down the trauma from my past in the busy moments of being a wife and mom. My marriage soon fell apart and so did I. I found myself alone with three children, feeling rejected and suffocating from the pain of the past and a broken relationship. I honestly wanted to give up.

"During that time, I received a letter from Calvary's Love church, offering to give my children Christmas gifts. I thought it was a cool, safe place to have a family night and I loved it. One month later, I attended an all worship night. When I walked into the church, I instantly felt something different. That night, God said to me through someone else, 'Your story is not over. When Jesus was dying on the cross, they thought His story was over, but just as Jesus rose from the dead, the Lord wants you to know that your story is not over.' I knew that it meant something for me, but I didn't understand it all at that moment. I committed to myself that I would be back. God was there, and I knew it. A few months later, I accepted Christ into my heart and surrendered my whole life to Jesus. He has made Himself so incredibly real to me that I cannot fully put it into words.

"Since that day, my life is completely transformed. The biggest thing is that God healed me from the pain of my past! Now I am set free from the thoughts that shamed me and made me feel so filthy! I have never felt so clean and refreshed. This change has happened only by the power of the Holy Spirit. I discovered that He loved me and longed for me. Not the fixed Jasmine, but just the way I was: broken and ashamed. When I cast all my cares on Him, He brought me so much rest. He set me free. I am truly free."

Since then, Jasmine has come to know Jesus to be her Everything. Jasmine is radiant with God's peace and joy. She is walking in her God-given calling to make disciples as she brings the hope and healing of Jesus to other broken women and single moms. To God be the glory!

We have seen many lives rescued and restored by the love of Jesus. Though the gifts have opened doors and been a blessing in many ways, it is not necessarily about the gifts; it's about loving people. This outreach has also opened the door for other outreach opportunities within the school.

God birthed a dream in us many years ago to open a community center offering afterschool care, and other outreach activities in our city. Last year He miraculously provided a building for us and the school is busing children to our afterschool program. Many of the same youth we are investing in at the program are integrating into our church's youth group and the downtown presence of this building is giving us more opportunities to connect with the community.

The Adoption Approach

We first met Dee and her two daughters at our annual park outreach several years ago. Every year, she promised to come to a church service, but was never able to make it. We met her again at the "Love Gift" night. "I am in a dark pit, and I just can't get out," she used to say. This is her story:

"It was about the fourth time I attended the park outreach, feeling overwhelmed and despair about my life. Someone prayed with me and I surrendered my life to the Lord. God said, 'If you stay with these people, they will teach you about Me.' Though I did not come to church right away, it was the start of a new beginning because I received hope. God also showed me I needed Him to overcome my alcohol addiction."

Kookie, one of our church members, "adopted" Dee and her girls by giving her daughters a ride every Wednesday to our kids' clubs. She started building a friendship with Dee, keeping in regular contact with her and helping the family in various ways. Through this relationship of genuine care and concern, Dee finally came. God brought her out of that dark pit and she and her family became part of our church. She was water baptized and completed our New Beginnings group for new believers. Dee was transformed by the love and power of God. She rebuilt her relationship with the father of her children and they got married. Kookie continues to encourage Dee and her family in their walk with Christ.

Matt was an introverted and lonely child. Diane first met him when she was appointed as his personal aide in elementary school. He had many emotional needs. He struggled for love in his broken home and carried the stress of it to school each day. Looking for a way to connect with him, Diane found out that Matt wanted to learn how to swim. She wanted to help him start lessons, but needed his mother's permission to take him to swimming lessons. Not long after Diane prayed for God to make a way, Matt's mom walked into the classroom with cupcakes. Diane took the opportunity to introduce herself and ask if she could take Matt for swimming lessons. His surprised mom responded, "Why would you do that?" Without hesitation, Diane explained, "I'm a single parent. My husband passed away when my children were very young. There were times when people helped me, and I was so blessed by their acts of kindness that I wanted to be able to do the same someday. As the teacher's aide in Matt's class, I've enjoyed getting to know him, and he's been telling me about how he wants to learn how to swim. He said he doesn't have someone to take him because you're at work. I'd like to take him."

Dropping Matt off at his home after swimming lessons each week helped her build trust with Matt's mom. Diane cared deeply for this eight-year-old boy and his mother, wanting them to know Jesus.

Sometime later, Matt's mom agreed that Diane could bring him to our church's Wednesday night kids' clubs, and later in the year, someone sponsored him to go to summer camp with our church. The teachers at school commented on how they saw positive changes in Matt and offered to help sponsor him to go to camp the following year where Matt accepted Christ! The end of Matt's story has not been written yet, but we know there is a strong foundation invested in his life.

There are many fatherless children who need a positive role model in their lives. It can make an enormous difference when we include them in our family activities, exposing them to the life of Christian family. It may be their first introduction to what God intended family to be. In our church, we also have several families who felt led by God to adopt a child permanently. This parallels our own spiritual adoption by Christ into His family. There are children all over the United States and across the world who are desperately in need of a family. You may spiritually "adopt" a child, a teen, or an adult, welcoming them into your life and connecting them to your

Savior. Bring them to church, invite them to dinner, or help meet a need. That's where it begins.

There are many more ways we have found to be effective for sharing the gospel with different populations. This includes visitation to those in nursing homes and those who are incarcerated, providing a live free ministry, a transportation ministry to provide rides to church, as well as opening a food pantry and clothing closet. It is important to follow the leading of the Holy Spirit for you as an individual or as a church in choosing the method or approach to show the love of Jesus and share the gospel with those around you and abroad.

As I mentioned earlier, we often have the opportunity to connect with those whom we meet "along our way," but God has also called us to reach those who are "out of our way." While ministering in a women's prison during one of our missions trips to Ecuador, God deeply moved in LuAnn's heart. On our flight home, LuAnn told me she felt called to minister to women who were incarcerated. She came to see me after we got home, having received Isaiah 61 as confirmation. It was the same scripture God had given us years ago and it had been on our heart to have a ministry in the local jails.

LuAnn joined a minister who was doing jail services and found the women who attended very receptive. God has opened many doors and she now leads a team of twelve ladies who regularly minister in the jail providing church services. God comes in powerful ways and the women worship and often weep, moved by the presence of the Holy Spirit. It is now called "Inside Out Ministry," has grown through the years, and includes counseling and aftercare mentoring. Through this ministry, many women have found Jesus as Savior and are reaching out to others.

This is Jeannine's story:

"It was a dark day when my mother died at age 9. My life was marked with emotional, mental, and physical abuse all growing up. When my father died from alcohol abuse when I was 15, I became homeless. Looking for love in all the wrong places, I got involved with the wrong people. I moved in with a woman to help take care of her two kids. I was sex trafficked at age 17 by a neighbor who pointed a gun to my head while staying at a hotel with my fiancé. This man told me he had total control over my life and I was ordered to go with him. I was scared and afraid I would die if I did not obey him. By a miracle of God, I was able to escape at a gas station. To numb my intense pain, I used drugs and I became a heroin dealer. This became my way of life for many years and I was headed down a dark, very lonely path. I felt broken and ripped to the core.

"When I was serving time in jail, I met Pastor LuAnn, director of 'Inside Out' Jail ministry. I went to the services she was leading and felt something new and different. I saw faith in God renewed and lives restored. In my hopelessness, I had planned to overdose on heroin, but instead, I collapsed when I felt the overflowing love from God. In that moment, God renewed my worth and desire to live. My life was radically changed as I repented from all my sin, and completely surrendered my life to Jesus. He redeemed me, and my eyes were opened to His purpose for my life. My God is amazing, and He made all things new!"

Jeannine is overflowing with the love, peace, and joy of Jesus, ministering to women who are broken and wounded. She serves as a leader with our 'Live Free' ministry, an addiction recovery program, and recently has joined our church staff.

God has even opened more doors. Carol ministers to women who are incarcerated in a different county jail. More women are hearing the good news about Jesus in other counties and, through Him, lives are being transformed. It is not always easy and sometimes it seems impossible, but God continues to confirm His Word with miracles.

Our nursing home outreach team finds great joy visiting the elderly in a local nursing home. Many of the residents are lonely and heartbroken, having lost their homes, possessions, and spouses. God has called us to bring the hope of Jesus to the brokenhearted. This outreach also opens the door to connect with family members who are visiting, along with staff members. Kathy, our nursing home team coordinator, recently told me a story about one of the residents.

"We met Ruth, a Jewish lady, who had faith in God but not in Jesus as the living, miracle-working Son of God. After a few visits, our team had the opportunity to pray with Ruth. We prayed for physical healing, for a recliner (as she was unable to sleep in the bed), and for family conflicts to be resolved. At the next visit, our team walked in and saw a new recliner in the room. When she was asked where it came from, she said, 'Some men just brought it in!' Her physical issues were better and the conflicts in her family were resolved. After this answer to prayer, Ruth became open to learning about Jesus and requested a Bible. Recently, we had the opportunity to show her and many other residents, the movie *A Case for Christ* and discussed the movie afterwards. Ruth loved the movie and started reading the New Testament. Just the other day Ruth was rushed to the hospital with a respiratory collapse, in ICU and on a ventilator. She was not expected to live. When we came to visit, she told us with tears in her eyes, "I heard a voice saying, you will be going home soon". She knew it was not the staff or her family speaking. She then felt a comforting hand on her back and heard the same voice saying, "You will be able to speak now. Ruth believes it was the presence of Jesus that got her through this trying time. She asked if she could attend our church. We can't wait to see all that God is going to do in her life!"

We continue to declare that "The Spirit of the Lord God is upon [us] because the Lord has anointed [us] to preach good tidings to the poor. He has sent [us] to heal the brokenhearted, to proclaim liberty to the captives and the opening of the prison to those who are bound. To proclaim the acceptable year of the Lord…To comfort all who mourn…to give them beauty for ashes, the oil of joy for mourning, the garment of praise for the spirit of heaviness. That they may be called trees of righteousness, the planting of the Lord, that He may be glorified. And they shall rebuild the old ruins. They shall raise up the former desolations. And they shall repair the ruined cities. The desolations of many generations" (Isaiah 61:1-4, NKJV).

Through the Holy Spirit, God will help us to be creative in reaching out. The purpose for these various approaches is not for us to pick one that we are most comfortable with, but to be

> The purpose for these various approaches is not for us to pick one that we are most comfortable with, but to be open to the Holy Spirit to use us however He chooses.

open to the Holy Spirit to use us however He chooses. He knows the way to a person's heart and what it takes to reach them. *Salvation **is** and **remains** the work of the Spirit and He is faithful to lead us!*

Continue to pray and be aware of the treasurers around you, seeing and loving the one in front of you and being intentional about how you choose to be His witness.

"I do not consecrate myself to be a missionary or a preacher. I consecrate myself to God to do His will where I am, be it in school, office or kitchen, or wherever He may, in His wisdom, send me" (Watchman Nee).

"I used to ask God to help me. Then I asked if I might help Him. I ended up by asking Him to do His work through me" (Hudson Taylor).

REFLECTIONS AND APPLICATION

1. What speaks to you from Jesus' approach, witnessing to Nicodemus (John 3:1-21) and the Samaritan woman (John 4:4-42) and from Paul's approach to the people in Athens (Acts 17:16-34)?

2. People need to feel we genuinely value and care for them no matter how they respond. Why is this important in every approach we take?

3. Which of the approaches described do you find most appealing to use? Why? Which of the approaches described do you find most challenging? Why?

4. Why is it so important not to adopt just a single approach, but to allow the Holy Spirit to prompt us as to the best approach for each situation?

5. Every story is the proof the world is waiting to see; therefore, your story is important! Take a few minutes to reflect on the following: What prayers has God been answering in your life? What new things are you learning in God's Word? In what way have you been transformed? What difference has Christ made in your life and circumstances?

6. In what way does the idea that we are not responsible for convincing others of the reality of God enable you to more freely approach people?

7. After this teaching, what steps will you take to become more comfortable as an instrument of the Holy Spirit, open to be used in whatever way He chooses to use you in sharing the gospel?

6

THE MESSAGE

Living the Message

Jesus not only *spoke* the message of the gospel, He *lived* the message before the people. He *was* the message sent from God! "In the beginning was the Word, and the Word was with God, and the Word was God… The Word became flesh and made His dwelling among us… full of grace and truth" (John 1:1, 14).

Philip asked Jesus, "Show us the Father…" Jesus answered, "Philip… anyone who has seen Me, has seen the Father…" (John 14:8-10). He basically says to Philip, "When you encounter Me, you encounter your Father." This is both a powerful response and powerful example for us to follow. Jesus revealed the Father to those He encountered, and God has chosen you and me to make Him known to the world. When people interact with us, they should have an opportunity to see Jesus and have an encounter with Him. God's people are the expression and extension of His eyes, hands, and feet—His body in a world lost in darkness.

God's people are the expression and extension of His eyes, hands, and feet—His body in a world lost in darkness.

Sometime ago, my son-in-law Steve came home heavy-hearted. It had been a pressure-filled week at work where he is the Regional Vice President of the company he works for. Many of us can relate to the demands and challenges in the work place. "The values and ethics of some of the men I work with are just so different and it gets difficult at times. Everything is fast paced, and I don't know how I could reach them."

Together with his wife, Jaime, they prayed for his colleagues and for strength to live out the life of Christ before them. The following week, one of the executives asked Steve about his family and this opened the door for Steve to tell about some of his challenges. He simply explained that the challenges in his life had made them stronger in their faith in God and that all they could do is give their situation into the hands of God. As a result, this executive opened up to Steve about challenges with his son who has been suffering from leukemia for six years. Steve listened attentively as this dear man spoke with tears in his eyes, confiding in him about his personal pain for his son. This had never happened before, and Steve was amazed. In his own words, "I was thankful God opened the door to encourage my colleague and share with him how the Lord had been my strength, bringing me and my family through a time of impossibility. I was also encouraged how God can just open the door to share about Him, if I remain faithful to live the life of Jesus and His integrity and love before them. I was definitely looking forward to another opportunity to have a follow-up conversation with him and was trusting God for more open doors. However, the other day, this same man *approached me* about a different heartache in his life. My heart filled with compassion for him. As he confided in me, I had another opportunity to talk with him and was able to pray with him, which strengthened and encouraged him."

Sometimes people will approach us with questions because they are drawn to the light of Christ in us. The life of Jesus within us is the light. "In Him was life, and that life was the light of men" (John 1:4). He has told us that we are now the light of the world. "You're here to be light, bringing out the God-colors in the world. God is not a secret to be kept. We're going public with this, as public as a city on a hill. If I make you light-bearers, you don't think I'm going to hide you under a bucket, do you? I'm putting you on a light stand. Now that I've put you there on a hilltop, on a light stand — shine! Keep open house, be generous with your lives. By opening up to others you'll prompt people to open up with God, this generous Father in heaven" (John 8:12, Matthew 5:14-15 MSG).

When people see the message of the gospel lived out, it helps them to understand what it looks like to be a follower of Jesus. Paul was communicating this message to the believers in Corinth: "You show that you are a letter from Christ... known and read by everybody" (2 Corinthians 3:3-2). God's people are often the only 'story of Jesus' read by those around us. Alton Garrison puts it this way: "The revelation of Jesus comes to your family and to those in your work place when they see the Word of God in action."[4] Paul states, "... Our gospel came to you not simply with words, but also with power, with the Holy Spirit and with deep conviction. You know how we lived among you for your sake (1 Thessalonians 1:5).

Knowing the Message

Jesus' death on the cross and His resurrection from the dead has made salvation possible. He opened the door to the Father for everyone who repents of sin and believes in Him. Isaiah's prophecy paints a clear picture of Jesus' sacrifice and the purpose for which He came and died.

> "But He was pierced for our transgressions, He was crushed for our iniquities, the punishment that brought us peace was upon Him, and by His wounds we are healed" (Isaiah 53:5).

> "We all, like sheep, have gone astray, each of us has turned to his own way, and the Lord has laid on Him the iniquity of us all . . . because He poured out His life unto death, and was numbered with the transgressors. For He bore the sins of many and made intercession for the transgressors" (Isaiah 53:6, 12).

In his powerful message on the day of Pentecost, Peter speaks about Jesus' resurrection from the dead.

> "But God raised Him from the dead, freeing Him from the agony of death, because it was impossible for death to keep its hold on Him...God has raised this Jesus to life, and we are all witnesses of this fact" (Acts 2:24, 32).

We can selflessly serve people, invite them to church, and share our story with others. However, ultimately, they need to hear the good news of the gospel to be saved.

What is the gospel message? Gospel means "good news." In brief, the good news is that Jesus came to save us from sin, so that we can live in relationship with God now and forever. Do we grasp this? The life Jesus lives, right now, in relationship with the Father, is available to us. But why? Because God saw a lost world with lost people forever separated from Him because of sin—people just like you and I—who needed a Savior.

He loved us so much He sent His Son Jesus to rescue us. You see, God knew no matter how hard we tried to rescue ourselves, we would always fall short. He knew our best efforts to be good or get to Him wouldn't be enough, so *He* came to us! Jesus came to the world to die for our sin and restore what was lost and broken. Through the shed blood of Christ, His death and resurrection, He's offering all who repent of their sin and believe in His name the right to be called children of God, the gift of eternal life, and the power to live as Christ lived by His Spirit.

Knowing the message of the gospel enables you to be prepared to present it when the opportunity arises. Understanding the power of this message also strengthens your confidence as you share it.

The Power of the Message

"Christ... sent me to preach the gospel—not with words of human wisdom lest the cross of Christ be emptied of its power. For the message of the cross is foolishness to those who are perishing, but to us who are being saved it is the power of God" (1 Corinthians 1:17-18).

Chip and Cindy came walking into our church one Sunday morning. I recognized Cindy to be the lady who had raised her hand for salvation the previous Wednesday and remembered she had not come to the prayer room for follow-up. I grabbed a salvation packet and sat down next to our new guests. After introductions and rejoicing about Cindy's salvation, I asked if I could explain to her about the gift of salvation. She eagerly agreed. Noticing her husband next to Cindy, I held out the booklet I was using far enough so both could follow along. I simply explained the message of God's purpose for a personal relationship with Jesus Christ. When finished, I asked Cindy if it made sense.

To my surprise, her husband Chip immediately responded, "That makes a lot of sense." The message of the cross is the power of God unto salvation! Chip heard the message and responded to receive and believe it, as well! They both committed their lives to Jesus. That night, Chip slept through the night for the first time in 25 years. Ever since returning from service in the Vietnam War, Chip had battled night terrors and post-traumatic stress effects. This sent him into a whirlwind of alcoholism and family problems as he tried to cope with his inner turmoil. That day, he was miraculously healed and restored, which led to the healing of his marriage and family relationships. We were thrilled that this precious couple joined God's family. Since then, they have been involved as leaders in our church, serving Jesus with all their hearts!

The message of the cross not only involves truth, but has power to redeem from sin's power, heal, and deliver from every chain of bondage. "For the kingdom of God is not a matter of talk, but of power" (1 Corinthians 4:20). It is not complicated. The message of the cross is so simple that anyone can understand it!

The message of the cross not only involves truth, but has power to redeem from sin's power, heal, and deliver from every chain of bondage.

Communicating the Message

Romans 10:14-15 tells us of the importance of *communicating His message* with those who do not know Him. "How then, can they call on the one they have not believed in? And how can they believe in the one of whom they have not heard? And how can they hear without someone preaching to them?"

Cornelius and his family believed in God, prayed regularly, and gave to those in need. However, he did not know the message of the Lord Jesus Christ. God heard his prayer and sent an angel to tell him to connect with Peter, who would tell him the message. In the same breath the angel told Cornelius about Peter, he could have told him about Jesus. Though God uses angels for specific purposes, He has ordained that His church share the good news of Jesus Christ. God went out of His way, as He always does, to connect Peter with Cornelius! He specifically joined these two men, who otherwise would not have been in the same house or even in the same conversation. While Peter was praying, God prepared him through a vision. When Peter came to the house of Cornelius, he found the entire family and many close friends whom Cornelius had also eagerly invited. They already knew that Jesus had come for the Jews, but did not know the good news that Jesus had come for them, as well.

Many people in our culture are either religious or have heard about Jesus in one way or another, but do not know how the powerful message of Jesus applies to them personally. Of course, there are also millions in the world today who have never heard of the name of Jesus.

Peter received the revelation right then, that God sent Jesus for *every* person of *every* nation. Let's walk through Peter's explanation of the gospel in this instance.

- Peter talked with Cornelius and asked some questions before he shared the message of the gospel (Acts 10:27-33).

- He told them about the good news of peace available through Jesus Christ, who is Lord of all (Acts 10:36).

- He simply talked about who Jesus was and the powerful works He had done (Acts 10:37-39).

- He then told about Jesus dying on the cross and being raised from the dead. Peter shared he knew this to be true, because he had personally encountered Jesus and ate and drank with Him (personal relationship) (Acts 10:34-41). When you speak about the message of the cross, you and

I can also identify with this reality by sharing about our personal relationship, encounters, or experiences with Jesus, which give proof of His death and resurrection.

> When you speak about the message of the cross, you and I can also identify with this reality by sharing about our personal relationship, encounters, or experiences with Jesus.

- Peter finished the message by emphasizing, "Everyone who believes in Him receives forgiveness of sins through His name" (Acts 10:43). Peter had personally experienced forgiveness in a powerful way for denying the name of Jesus. When we personally have experienced His forgiveness and have been set free, we want others to experience the glory of being forgiven, as well.

- While Peter was still speaking these words, the Holy Spirit came on all who heard the message (Acts 10:44).

You may wonder, can I truly lead a person to Christ? When it comes down to it, what do I really need to say to help them understand the free gift of salvation? How do I start?

Over 20 years ago I learned about "Steps to Peace with God" by the Billy Graham Association. I started using it when sharing the gospel. Over the years I developed my own way of sharing it and below is a description of that. Yet I realize it was shaped by what I learned long ago. Let's break the gospel message down into simple steps.

God's Plan: God loves you and has a special plan for your life. He has promised peace and life through a personal relationship with Him, now and forever.

> "But God so loved the world that He gave His one and only Son, that whoever believes in Him shall not perish but have eternal life" (John 3:16).

> "...We have peace with God through our Lord Jesus Christ" (Romans 5:1).

Our Problem: The wrong things we have done (sin) separate us from a Holy God. The root word for sin means *"to miss the mark."* We have all been born in sin, missed the mark, and fallen short of His holiness. The result of sin is physical and spiritual death, separation from God forever.

> "For all have sinned and fall short of the glory of God" (Romans 3:23).

> "For the wages of sin is death, but the gift of God is eternal life in Christ Jesus our Lord" (Romans 6:23).

God's Solution: God loves us more than we can imagine. He did not want to be separated from us. He did everything to redeem us. God sacrificed His Son Jesus who paid the penalty for our sins by dying on the cross in our place and rose from the grave. He offers us a new life, one that is united with God in true relationship.

"But God demonstrates his own love for us in this: While we were still sinners, Christ died for us" (Romans 5:8).

"I am the way and the truth and the life. No one comes to the Father except through me" (John 14:6).

Our Choice: The gift of life now and forever through Jesus can be ours, if we choose to receive Jesus for ourselves. Believe that He is the Son of God and that He died for you. Be willing to repent of your sin and ask Him to forgive you. It's not enough to know it; you need to trust and receive Jesus as your Savior.

"That if you confess with your mouth, 'Jesus is Lord' and believe in your heart that God raised Him from the dead, you will be saved" (Romans 10:9).

"In Him we have redemption through His blood, the forgiveness of sins, in accordance with the riches of God's grace" (Ephesians 1:7).

"Yet to all who received Him, to those who believed in His name, He gave the right to become children of God" (John 1:12).

Prayer

"Dear Lord Jesus, thank You for Your great love. I understand that my sins have separated me from You. I do not want to be separated from You, so I ask You to forgive me. Thank You for dying on the cross for all my sins. I believe that You are Jesus the Son of the living God and that You were raised from the dead. I invite You to come into my heart and life and I trust You as my Lord and Savior. Thank You for loving me and I want to follow You the rest of my life. In Jesus' name, Amen."

Assurance: Once you have obeyed the Scriptures to surrender your life to Christ and repent (turn away from your sins and toward Christ), you have the assurance of eternal life because now you are a child of God.

> The payment is the very life of Jesus which has been made in full, so you can stop striving to be saved and rest in the saving power of Jesus Christ.

All of your sins, your debts, and your failures were nailed to the cross with Christ (Colossians 2:14), and all of Christ's righteousness is placed upon you (2 Corinthians 5:21). You are in right standing with God; you are redeemed (restored to a relationship with God by means of a payment). The payment is the very life of Jesus which has been made in full, so you can stop striving to be saved and rest in the saving power of Jesus Christ. He has completed it for you and now your relationship with God can continue to grow as you get to know Him more.

"God has given us eternal life, and this life is in his Son. He who has the Son has life, he who does not have the Son of God does not have life. I write these things to you who believe in the name of the Son of God so that you may know that you have eternal life" (1 John 5:11-13).

"For it is by grace you have been saved, through faith—and this not from yourselves, it is the gift of God—not by works, so that no one can boast" (Ephesians 2:8-9).

"Therefore, if anyone is in Christ, he is a new creation, the old has gone, the new has come" (2 Corinthians 5:17).

The Clarity of the Message

Bethany sincerely prayed to receive Christ into her heart upon hearing an invitation one Sunday morning. Though she accepted Christ, she felt discouraged she did not have the same faith and dedication to Jesus as her other believing friends who had been serving the Lord for a long time.

As Bethany shared this with me at a women's event, I asked her if she truly understood the gospel. When she confirmed it was unclear, I offered to share it with her. She loved hearing the good news of the gospel and drank in every word. The parable of the sower also came to mind, so I shared it with her. We realized from this parable that she had been like the one who had received the seed along the path. Jesus explains that some hear the message about the kingdom but do *not understand* it. The evil one then comes and snatches away what was sown in his heart. This is the seed sown along the path (Matthew 13:4, 19).

When I told Bethany the meaning of the parable, she was pleasantly surprised to recognize herself in this story. Now that she clearly understood the powerful gospel message, we prayed the prayer of salvation again and she was literally set free on the spot! After receiving clarity, she was excited to learn that God had a purpose just for her. She was beginning her own special journey with God and did not need to compare her faith to that of others.

As we prepare ourselves to share a clear explanation of the gospel, we can also pray that God enables us in that moment. Paul encourages us to pray with expectation for open doors, but also for *clarity* to speak His message.

"Devote yourselves to prayer, being watchful and thankful. And pray for us, too, that God may open a door for our message, so that we may proclaim the mystery of Christ, for which I am in chains. Pray *that I may proclaim it clearly, as I should.* Be wise in the way you act toward outsiders, make the most of every opportunity. Let your conversation be always full of grace, seasoned with salt, so that you may know how to answer everyone" (Colossians 4:2-6).

It is also important to avoid using Christian language unfamiliar to those outside of the church, and remember, it often takes several seeds before the person commits to Christ.

Confirming the Message

Some believers have wondered how they can assure a person of the truth of this message. This is not our task. This is the work of the Holy Spirit, who is also called the Spirit of truth (John 14:17). He

Himself will bear witness of the truth that you speak, just as He did with Peter in the house of Cornelius.

"The Spirit Himself bears witness with our spirit that we are children of God" (Romans 8:16, NKJV).

As I shared the good news of Jesus with Becky, a Jewish lady, I felt the Spirit was drawing her, though she hesitated. The Holy Spirit gave me insight about her hesitation. I said, "You are wondering, 'How can I know Esther is speaking the truth about Jesus since many people claim to speak truth about their religion?'" With confidence I responded, "You just know deep down in your heart I am speaking the truth, for the scriptures says, 'that the Spirit Himself will bear witness of the truth.'"

Happily surprised, Becky acknowledged this was exactly what she had been thinking and it confirmed truth to her! We prayed together, and I left her with scripture that explained it well.

In the approach chapter, we discussed various ways to approach a person, God's special treasure. We begin by noticing the one in front of us and showing genuine care through conversation to those 'on our way' and reach out to the one 'out of our way.' We listen sincerely to what they are saying, ask genuine questions, and at the same time, pray for God to open the door to speak about Him. We are sensitive to what God is orchestrating and join Him in what He is doing. When I am engaged in conversation and God is opening the door to share the

> We are sensitive to what God is orchestrating and join Him in what He is doing.

gospel, I speak about the reality of my personal relationship with Jesus Christ and what this means to me just as Peter did. In other words, we share our own story (there is more discussion about this in chapter five).

I often explain the difference between religion and relationship with Christ. In other words, religion is men climbing up the mountain on different paths hoping to find the assurance of God on top of the mountain. True relationship with Christ is God coming down the mountain, seeking for us and giving His life in death on the cross that we might be forgiven and live with Him forever.

As stated earlier, many people have religious beliefs and are still searching for the truth, waiting for the one who can satisfy the void in their lives, and not realizing He has come! He came! He died for our sins so that we might be forgiven. When He died, He cried out, "It is finished!" He desperately longs for every person to know His true purpose. We are born to have a personal relationship with God through Jesus Christ His Son now and forever!

> In reaching this generation who is longing for relationship, it is a golden opportunity for the church to present the good news of a personal relationship with Jesus.

In reaching this generation who is longing for relationship, it is a golden opportunity for the church to present the good news of a personal relationship with Jesus. He desires for us to love Him with all our heart, soul, mind, and strength and love our neighbor as ourselves! It's not hard; it's simple. It requires our choice to acknowledge we are lost without Him and that we must receive forgiveness of our sins, receiving Jesus as Lord and Savior. As we share His message, the good news of the gospel, the Holy Spirit is the One who draws, convicts, and saves them!

"I planted the seed, Apollos watered it, *but God made it grow*. So, neither he who plants nor he who waters is anything, but only God, who makes things grow. The man who plants and the man who waters have one purpose, and each will be rewarded according to his own labor. We are God's fellow workers, you are God's field, God's building" (1 Corinthians 3:6-9).

REFLECTION AND APPLICATION

1. What speaks to you from the story of Peter witnessing to Cornelius (Acts 10:1-44)?

2. What does it mean to "live out the gospel message?"

3. Why is it so damaging for believers to live one way in Christ and another throughout the week? What message is that portraying to our families, our friends, and the world?

4. In your own words, how would you explain the gospel?

5. How has the gospel message personally transformed you?

6. Is there any part of the gospel that has been unclear to you before now? Or has there been any part of the gospel that you've struggled to share?

7. What is the difference between religion and relationship?

8. What steps will you take this week to share the gospel message with someone?

7

THE HELPER

As believers, we know the Great Commission. We know it was Jesus' final mandate to the church. We realize it is our responsibility to go into the world and share the good news with all and live on mission with God. Yet, knowing it and feeling able to actually *do* it are two separate things.

You may feel like I did when I was a teenager: "I know I want to share about Jesus and I know God wants me to do it. I certainly do not want people to be lost forever, but I feel inadequate and I just can't!"

Jesus did not just *command* us to be His witness. He gave the commandment with a promise: "You will receive *power* when the Holy Spirit comes on you, and you will be my witnesses in Jerusalem, and in all Judea and Samaria and to the ends of the earth" (Acts1:8). This power and boldness is demonstrated through the early church in the book of Acts and is still available to every believer today. Peter, who had been too fearful to stand with Christ during His arrest, boldly proclaimed to a big crowd on the day of

> This power enables you to do what you cannot and to be what you are not, because He is your Helper.

Pentecost: "The promise (of the Holy Spirit) is for you and your children and for all who are far off—for all whom the Lord our God will call" (Acts 2:39).

This power enables you to do what you cannot and to be what you are not, because He is your Helper. You do not have to do it alone! The apostle Paul depended on this power: "I came to you in weakness and fear, and with much trembling. My message and my preaching were not with wise and persuasive words, but with a demonstration of the *Spirit's power,* so that your faith might not rest on men's wisdom, but on God's power" (1 Corinthians 2:3-5). Jesus spoke concerning the Holy Spirit:

> "Nevertheless, I tell you the truth. It is to your advantage that I go away; for if I do not go away, the Helper will not come to you, but if I depart, I will send Him to you. And when He has come, He will convict the world of sin, and of righteousness and of judgment, of sin because they do not believe in Me, of righteousness, because I go to My Father and you see Me no more, of judgment because of the ruler of this world is judged" (John 16:7-11, NKJV).

The Holy Spirit Himself is actively drawing people to Jesus as we present the good news of the gospel. What an encouragement!

Susan came into our prayer room after the church service to commit her life to Jesus. When I asked her if this was the first time she was doing this, she confirmed it was and explained it had been quite a journey. She recognized God had been drawing her for a long time. She told me she felt this desire for God so intensely that she decided to go to a church to find out more about the reality of Jesus. That same week, her employer told her he was planning to check out Calvary's Love Church. She concluded this was God showing her where to go.

While wiping away her tears, Susan told me how she kept sensing God drawing her even throughout the entire service and therefore wanted to respond when the invitation was given to accept Christ. Jesus says, "I will draw all men ... No one can come to Him unless the Father... draws him" (John 12:32; 6:44). I further explained the Bible teaches us this drawing is not irresistible, for it can be rejected" (Matthew 23:37). Susan was very excited she had responded to Him. The desire and conviction resonating in her, which she recognized as the drawing of the Holy Spirit, showed her how much Jesus loved her and desired a personal relationship with her.

Philip's ministry in the book of Acts is a prime example of the work of the Holy Spirit (Acts 8:5-12). In a time of fierce persecution and hardship, Philip went down to a city in Samaria and proclaimed Christ there. Signs and wonders followed the preaching of the Word and the people believed, listening attentively to what Philip said. There was great joy in the city as a result of people turning to Christ.

"When the apostles in Jerusalem heard that Samaria had accepted the word of God, they sent Peter and John to them. When they arrived, they prayed for them that they might receive the Holy Spirit, because the Holy Spirit had not yet come upon any of them...Then, Peter and John placed their hands on them, and they received the Holy Spirit" (Acts 8:14-17).

The Holy Spirit gives you boldness and confidence to speak. As you speak, the Spirit is drawing and convicting the person to whom you are speaking. Even when the person does not respond immediately, many times He continues drawing him. When the person responds, the Holy Spirit Himself gives him the assurance that his sins are forgiven, and that Jesus truly is his Savior!

Mary sat across the table from me in our new believers' class pouring out her story. "The first time I participated in a service with Calvary's Love church I was so moved. I didn't even understand why, but I was weeping, overwhelmed by God's love. It's like I didn't want to leave, to move; I didn't want it to end. When I heard the invitation to begin a relationship with Jesus and ask His forgiveness, I knew it was for me because I felt convicted of my sin." I've heard a similar story often in our new believers' class. This is the work of the Holy Spirit.

The Holy Spirit in Action

As Philip was preoccupied with successful meetings and the breakout of true revival in Samaria, an angel of the Lord suddenly directed him to go down the desert road from Jerusalem to Gaza. In this story, we see how Philip kept following the prompting of the Spirit who led him. The Holy Spirit completely set up a perfect opportunity for Philip to share Jesus with one man who had come all the way from Ethiopia, to Jerusalem, desperately seeking to worship the true God (Acts 8:27).

Though God commands us to share Christ with the world, I am reminded again of the fact that God orchestrates opportunities for us to connect with one person who is seeking. We can

The Holy Spirit is already at work in preparing the hearts of those with whom we are to connect.

also believe and pray the Holy Spirit is already at work in preparing the hearts of those with whom we are to connect.

Just as the Holy Spirit prompted Philip to connect with the eunuch in a deserted place, the Holy Spirit is still at work today. God is looking for a person who is willing and open to the prompting of the Spirit as He desires to connect you and I to someone in need of the Savior!

Philip was flexible and willing to follow the leading of the Holy Spirit. On his way, he noticed a man riding in a chariot. The Spirit directed him to go near it. Philip obeyed the voice of the Spirit, but really did not know what would happen next. God may never ask you to 'join a chariot with an African eunuch,' but has He placed a neighbor, a co-worker, or a family member on your heart to connect with and walk with for a while? Who is on your path?

As Philip obeyed, he heard the eunuch reading from the book of Isaiah. Philip asked if he understood what he was reading, to which the man replied, "'How can I, unless someone explains it to me?'" The man asked Philip to come up and sit with him. "Then Philip opened his mouth, and beginning at this Scripture, preached Jesus to him" (Acts 8:30-35 NKJV). There are many people in our culture today who have some kind of knowledge of Christ, but lack the understanding of how the gospel applies to them personally. They need someone to explain it to them. Let's look at the role of the Holy Spirit in Philip's encounter.

- The Holy Spirit led Philip specifically to the eunuch.

- The Holy Spirit gave Philip the right words. He told him the good news of Jesus in such a clear way that the eunuch understood.

  "But the Helper, the Holy Spirit, whom the Father will send in My name, He will teach you all things, and bring to your remembrance all things that I said to you" (John 14:26, NKJV).

- The Holy Spirit convicted the eunuch.

  "And when He has come, He will convict the world of sin, and of righteousness and of judgment" (John 16:8, NKJV).

- The Holy Spirit drew this man.

  "I ... will draw all men to Myself" (John 12:32).

- The Holy Spirit gave Philip boldness.

  "But you will receive power when the Holy Spirit comes on you..." (Acts 1:8).

- The Holy Spirit gave the eunuch assurance and revelation that Jesus was the Son of God.

  "I believe that Jesus Christ is the Son of God" (Acts 8:37, NKJV).

  "But when He, the Spirit of truth comes, He will guide you into all truth" (John 16:13).

- The Holy Spirit's work resulted in great joy! (Acts 8:39).

  "The fruit of the Spirit is...joy" (Galatians 5:22).

The Helper was in action from beginning to end!

My father recalled the following powerful encounter:

"I was scheduled to have a series of outreach and ministry meetings on the island of Timor, Indonesia. A couple of weeks before my departure, one of the leaders called me, wondering if we should cancel because of a big fair that was scheduled during the same time. I told the leader that the Holy Spirit had led us to have these meetings, so we were not planning on canceling.

"God blessed this evangelism outreach and thousands attended! The Holy Spirit anointed His Word and confirmed it with signs and wonders as people were healed of all kinds of sicknesses and diseases such as asthma, arthritis, and ulcers. Crooked backs were made straight, the deaf could hear, and crippled people were able to walk. Not everyone had the opportunity to share his or her testimony publicly because so many people were healed. The power of God was present to heal.

"The night before the last meeting, I felt led to speak about the baptism of the Holy Spirit. The entire service was interpreted into their language. Following the message, I prayed, exalting the name of Jesus. Suddenly, the Holy Spirit fell, and the Lord literally filled thousands of people with the Holy Spirit. There were tears and shouts of joy! This heavenly joy was poured out in the hearts of thousands who had opened their hearts to Him. They were speaking in tongues as the Spirit gave them utterance. All hands were lifted high to praise and worship God. It was a mighty roaring sound that could be heard into the far distance. Though I had not spoken about healing, hundreds of people moved forward to share about God's mighty healing power in their bodies. Multitudes of people were saved and experienced the supernatural power of God. The meetings were so well attended, the authorities closed the fair."[5]

Though this happened many years ago, God is the same today! Jesus said through faith in Him, we would do the same works as He did and even greater things that the Father may be glorified (John 14:12-14).

Recently, my brother John went back to the same area to hold special meetings. An elderly man came to my brother with tears in his eyes sharing about the power of the Spirit that had been poured out long ago. He said, "Your father anointed me with oil forty-six years ago. I received God's power and anointing then, and I still feel that same anointing today!"

Scripture tells us of believers getting filled as they simply heard the Word of God spoken, just as the people did in Timor (Acts 10:44-46). Though most of the time, people received the Holy Spirit when someone prayed over them (Acts 8:15-17, 19:6).

My husband Jerry took a team from our church on a missions trip to Quito, Ecuador. He was scheduled to hold a series of meetings in Calvary's Love Church, which we helped build. On the last night, he spoke on the power of the Holy Spirit and many people came forward, hungry and expectant to receive more from God. His presence was tangible. Jerry and the team prayed for the people as they raised their hands, worshipping God. Tears flowed, and joy came over the entire congregation as many were filled with the Holy Spirit. It was a powerful experience and proof that He is still working and available today!

You may not have experienced the Holy Spirit in this same way, but He is ready and available as your Helper, Comforter, and Wisdom. I met Chantelle in the ladies' room of a hotel where we were staying for a minister's conference. As I was combing my hair by the sink, she initiated conversation with me about her work. The thought suddenly hit me, "Wow, this lady is very talkative. Maybe God is opening a door." I introduced myself and began to respond to her chatting. As she was walking out the door, I quickly told her that God loved her and wondered if she knew Him in personal relationship? Holding the door handle in her hand, she suddenly stopped and responded, "I used to go to church but haven't been in a long time. Life has been overwhelming and distracting." I knew Chantelle was in a bit of a hurry, but told her God led us to meet and asked her if I could just pray for her before she went back to work.

She eagerly accepted, and I prayed a simple prayer. However, the amazing thing is, that the Holy Spirit came powerfully in our midst during that prayer, right there in the ladies' room. It was the same Spirit who came in the big meeting in Timor, Indonesia, and the same Spirit's power who filled the people in Ecuador. He came in a mighty way and touched this woman in the core of her heart.

Tears streaming down her face, she was literally weeping in my arms! She knew without a doubt God had not forgotten her and He met her in a tangible way as He had lifted a heavy weight from her. She promised to go to church on Sunday and we exchanged emails, so I could send her some encouraging stories of hope. I was completely amazed and humbled about God's timing, leading, prompting, and wonderful presence of the Holy Spirit and how He had come in such a powerful way. To God be the glory!

I want to draw your attention once again to the scripture that simply states, "Philip opened his mouth"(Acts 8:35). In other words, the Holy Spirit literally directed his conversation with this diligent seeker. Philip was also prepared in his heart. He opened his mouth… out of his mouth came what was already in his heart. Paul said, "The word is near you; it is in your mouth and in your heart, that is, the word of faith we are proclaiming" (Romans 10:8). Our effective witness flows from our living relationship with Jesus (John 12:49-50). We can trust that when we open our mouth, the Spirit is faithful to give us the words that someone else needs (Luke 12:12). Each time this happens, I stand amazed about the words from the Spirit.

My dentist was engaged in an interesting conversation with his assistant while he was doing some work on my teeth. They were discussing different religions and how to prove which one was the true religion. I wondered what I would say, if I was asked about it. All of a sudden, the doctor said, "Don't worry, Esther, when we are done, I will give you an opportunity to give us your opinion." It made me realize how he was always open and interested to engage in such conversation. I started praying in my heart for the Spirit's wisdom to give me the right words to say. I knew I would only have time for one sentence, since the doctor would have to move on to his next patient—hardly enough time for such a big and important subject. I kept praying, "Holy Spirit, give me one sentence of truth to give proof that authentic Christianity is the true religion."

The Holy Spirit is always faithful to help us. While I was sitting with mouth open wide, He showed me what to say. When the dentist was all finished, he turned to me and said, "Well, Esther, what is your answer?"

I said, "The transformed lives of millions of people give proof that Jesus is alive and that He is the way, the truth, and the life."

The kind doctor quietly nodded as he sincerely listened and said goodbye. I am sure the words from the Holy Spirit gave him something to think about as he walked away to his next appointment.

How amazing that the Holy Spirit desires to direct us to a specific word, scripture, resource. . . or even an exact song to connect with certain people! This is my son Jerod's story:

"I was traveling to a church where I was invited to lead worship. As I drove, I began praying for the people who I would be ministering to that night. Praying for their lives, for their families, for their community. I didn't know them, but God knew them, and I needed to receive His heart. Suddenly, my prayers turned into a song and it felt as if the Holy Spirit began to literally sing through me, like I was a mouth piece and His words were pouring through my lips. The lyrics of the song felt more like a prayer and tears streamed down my face as I declared them. I can only imagine how concerned the other drivers on the road must've been as they drove by and saw me singing, snotting, and crying. I was a mess, but in that moment, I didn't care. I couldn't stop singing this new song that God had just written through me.

"Later that evening, I explained my experience with the people of this amazing church. I began singing the song and the whole church lifted their voices declaring the words that God had given just hours before. After the service, a group of pastors from the community approached me with wide eyes. They told me that for the past year they had been coming together as a community of church leaders for weekly prayer gatherings to believe God for their community. I was so encouraged, but what got my attention was what they told me next. They explained that the lyrics of the song that God had given were the exact words they had been praying each week!

...because they believed that the heart of God was to revive the 'dry bones' around them.

"Open hearts to what You promised
Break down walls of doubt that bind us
And pour it out
We won't rest until You fill us
Empowered to be Your witness

So pour it out, pour it out

We call out for You God to pour Your Spirit out

Revival consume us and raise these dry bones up"

"I could see faith and anticipation in these faithful pastors' eyes. They were giving their lives to a community that was dead and dark and seeing little fruit. They committed themselves to prayer because they believed that the heart of God was to revive the 'dry bones' around them. God used a song to confirm what He was speaking over their community. He used a simple servant like me to show them that they are seen and known by God, that He had not forgotten them, that He had not forgotten their community and that their prayers were heard from heaven."

The Holy Spirit was present from the beginning as He hovered over the waters and was striving with men (Genesis 1:2, 6:3). In the Old Testament, we read the Spirit came *upon* his servants at specific times. Jesus said His Spirit would come and live *within* us. "I will pray to the Father, and He will give you another Helper, that He may abide with you forever—the Spirit of truth, whom the world cannot receive, because it neither sees Him nor knows Him, but you know Him for He dwells *with* you and will be *in* you" (John 14:16-17, NKJV).

God has called us to live a life in the Spirit and has made every provision for us. He desires for the Spirit's power and anointing to overflow to every area of our lives. "Be filled with the Spirit" (Ephesians 5:18). Therefore, the Spirit does not only impart wisdom and power to *speak* for Him at specific moments, but He empowers us to *live* for Him continually. Simply put, He wants to

Simply put, He wants to *speak* through us and *live* through us! Isn't this amazing?

speak through us and *live* through us! Isn't this amazing? "His divine power has given us everything we need for life and godliness through our knowledge of Him who called us by His own glory and goodness" (2 Peter 1:3).

Through knowing and abiding in Jesus and His Word, His divine empowerment enables us to live Christ-like. The Spirit makes the presence of Jesus more real and His Word comes alive. To live in accordance with the Spirit is submitting ourselves to His guidance and relying on His power to live pleasing lives unto God. "For if you live according to the sinful nature, you will die; but if *by the Spirit* you put to death the misdeeds of the body, you will live, because those who are led by the Spirit of God, are sons of God" (Romans 8:13-14). In other words, we must depend on His Spirit to do what we cannot do ourselves. When the Spirit is truly at work in us, we will be more like Jesus in every way. This will increase our effectiveness as His witness to a world lost in darkness. "The fruit of the Spirit is love, joy, peace, patience, kindness, goodness, faithfulness, gentleness and self-control" (Galatians 5:22-23).

The Spirit empowers us to speak and live for Him, yet there are many additional blessings of the Holy Spirit. He comforts in our sorrows and sufferings and gives us power and authority to pray when we have no strength. Through the gifts of the Spirit, He gives us revelation knowledge beyond our own understanding, He imparts the gift of wisdom, lies are exposed, and God's truth is revealed. He gives us power to pray for the sick to be healed, fills us with faith that moves mountains, and calls us to join Him in supernatural miracles for the impossible still happening today (1 Corinthians 12:7-11).

We can depend on the Holy Spirit to open the right door and lead us as He did Philip on that desert road long ago. Come into His presence and ask God to fill you with the Holy Spirit. Through His Spirit you will receive His supernatural power, boldness, wisdom, guidance, and comfort in new and mighty ways. He *is* your Helper!

"If you then, though you are evil, know how to give good gifts to your children, how much more will your Father in heaven give the Holy Spirit to those who *ask* Him" (Luke 11:13).

REFLECTION AND APPLICATION

1. What speaks to you from the story of Philip and the eunuch? How can you apply what you have learned to your life and journey to spread the good news?

2. When Jesus commanded us to be His witness, He accompanied that command with the promise of the Holy Spirit. What does that promise mean to you?

3. The Holy Spirit is always actively at work drawing people to Jesus. How were you personally drawn by the Holy Spirit before you received Christ?

4. Describe how the Holy Spirit works with us as our Helper when it comes to witnessing.

5. How has the Holy Spirit helped you to share the gospel? If you've never shared the gospel, how does the knowledge of Him as Helper now embolden you to do so?

6. Has the Holy Spirit ever given you a word to share simply out of your obedience to "open your mouth"? If you've never experienced this before, in what way has your perspective now changed about following the promptings of the Holy Spirit to be His voice... even when you don't know what to say?

7. What steps will you take this week to come into His presence and be filled with the Spirit?

8

THE FOLLOW-UP

Bernard Johnson, missionary to Brazil, impacted my life thirty years ago in his passionate sermon about revival. "Do you know why we have revival in Brazil?" he asked. "We do not own comfortable buildings. We do not have the resources, curriculum, teachers, and preachers that other nations have, but we do have one thing. When someone gets saved, another believer walks the person down the aisle to the altar and keeps walking with this new believer until he becomes a true disciple of Jesus Christ. This is the reason we have revival in Brazil." I have never forgotten his words.

The fact is, those who come to Christ and have someone that can walk with them for a while have a far better chance of becoming disciples of Jesus than those who simply attend a church.

At our annual park outreach, we took the contact information of those who wanted to know God more and follow Jesus. My husband, Jerry, phoned Stella, who had given her life to Jesus at the park. She was moved that someone from our church would call her personally and she promised to visit our church services.

The following Sunday, she sat on the front row and God met her. When the speaker gave an invitation for salvation, Stella responded. Though she had received Christ at the park, she felt a need to do it again after she better understood what it meant. After a lady from our prayer team prayed with her, Stella came and found me, her face radiant with joy. "Can you tell your husband I was here today? He called me this week and I want to make sure he knows I came!" I assured her I would tell him and rejoiced with her about her new life in Jesus. Stella attended our small group for new believers where the leaders walked with her on this new journey. She shared this amazing story in small group:

"A couple of weeks ago, I got very discouraged because my car broke down and I was not able to get it fixed. I missed coming to church services and small group and started feeling disconnected from the church family as well as from God. During that time, I was also suffering from a bleed on my brain and felt very weak and overwhelmed. Sometime later, I attended our Christmas production rehearsal, though I was still very sick. During the prayer time before rehearsal, those who needed prayer were asked to come forward. I felt as if someone was literally pushing me to go. When others prayed for me, I felt God touching me in a powerful way. A few days later, I went back to my doctor and he was not able to find anything! God has done a huge miracle in me! Later that week, someone helped me with the car repairs. God is truly amazing and my provider in every way. I always bring my Bible to work and read it during my lunch break, which is helping me get closer to God. My co-worker's brother comes frequently to our shop, so I have gotten to know him. Sadly, I found out that he is a drug dealer and an addict. He has been asking questions about my new life in Christ and I have seen him peeking in my Bible. This week, he asked me for a Bible for himself. Surprisingly, he then asked me how he could get saved. I was thrilled but unsure I would be able to explain it well. I simply told him he had to repent of his sins because Jesus died for them on the cross and give his life over to Jesus. To my surprise, he wanted to do it! I am overwhelmed with what God is doing in my life! I am convinced He must have a great plan for me!"

Isn't this the purpose of discipleship, for disciples to make disciples? Even a new disciple can do this with God's help! An initial connection with a new believer may take place through something as a simple phone call, email, or text; however, the process of follow-up should lead to discipleship.

Just before Jesus ascended to heaven, He said, "All authority in heaven and earth has been given to Me. Therefore, go and *make disciples* of all nations, baptizing them in the name of the Father and of the Son and of the Holy Spirit, and teaching them to obey everything I have commanded you. And surely, I am with you always, to the very end of the age" (Matthew 28:18-20).

Jesus modeled this when He called the men who would become His disciples. "'Come, follow me,' Jesus said, 'and I will make you fishers of men'" (Matthew 4:19). He invited them to walk with Him and share a personal relationship with Him, so they could observe

> Discipleship is inviting someone to see and learn how to live in relationship with God (love God) and man (love others) according to God's Word.

and learn what it meant to be a *follower* of Jesus. He is asking us to do the same. Their faith in Him was not the only goal or the end result, but rather, it was the beginning. Discipleship is inviting someone to see and learn how to live in relationship with God (love God) and man (love others) according to God's Word. It is about the process of transformation in Christ-likeness in everyday life.

Relationship

Discipleship involves relationship. Relationships grow with time and require effort, but through them, new believers have the opportunity to see the evidence of Jesus in a real way. For new believers, the person of Jesus and His ways are relatively foreign. They have an entirely different perspective on life that has shaped over years of time and experience.

When they accept Christ, they become part of God's family. Therefore, as they begin the discipleship process, a relationship with another believer in the church family offers guidance and encouragement for their new life in Christ. We are all called to care for one another, just as the early church did in the book of Acts. "...You are members of God's very own family... and you belong in

God's household with every other Christian" (Ephesians 2:19 LB). Paul encouraged the Ephesians: "From Him the whole body, joined and held together by every supporting ligament, grows and builds itself up in love, as each part does its work" (Ephesians 4:16).

Charlene, a young mom, has a heart to connect with people in her world of influence, sharing Christ and inviting them to church services and events. She loves to allow God to use her to "walk with them" in their new-found faith. Every week while her daughter goes to dance lessons, she meets her friend at a local coffee shop to read and pray together. This is helping her friend learn how to believe and pray for her family. Charlene told me, "I actually receive myself from this time together with my friend. We end up encouraging each other." Truly, "…he who refreshes others will himself be refreshed" (Proverbs 11:25).

Marion is eighty years old and has been faithful to our prayer group for many years. God is using her to invest in some of the young women who have joined our group. You will often find Marion listening, talking, and praying with a young mom, long after our prayer time is over. They know they can call her to talk and pray when needed. Through her relationship with them, she is investing and making disciples for God's Kingdom.

Modeling

The Christian life is not just taught but "caught." We are called to live for Jesus in front of others. People don't just want to hear about it, they need to see and experience how it works. I first learned this as a young mom when my children were little. One day, the Lord showed me the verse in Deuteronomy 6:5-6 that says, "Love the Lord your God with all your heart and with all your soul and with all your strength. These commandments that I give you today are to be upon your hearts. Impress them on your children. Talk about them when you sit at home and when you walk along the road, when you lie down and when you get up." At first glance, I wondered how I could talk about these commandments 24-7 with my children? Then I realized besides teaching His ways, God intended for me to *"live it out"* as a life style in front of my children so they could "catch" it! Discipleship starts in the home.

This is exactly what Jesus did. As we observe His interaction with His disciples, we learn that for three and a half years, Jesus spent time with these twelve men, and they watched Him live in obedience to the Father. They saw how He loved the little children and embraced those who were broken. As they observed Jesus pray daily to His Father, they asked Him to teach them how to pray. They experienced the power of His Word as He rebuked the storm and were amazed when the winds and waves obeyed. Countless miracles of healing and deliverance were the everyday norm. As they obeyed His Word, their nets overflowed with fish and a small portion of food was multiplied to feed thousands when He prayed over it. They were surprised to see how He reached into the lives of those who were sinful and pursued the outcasts. They admired His humility as He took a towel and took the place of a servant. The disciples were forever changed as they witnessed how Jesus laid down His life on a daily basis even unto death. The model is a powerful teacher.

> The model is a powerful teacher.

God went out of His way to send Paul and his companions to Philippi where they met a group of ladies praying at the river. The Lord opened the heart of a business woman in the group named Lydia to respond to Paul's message and she and her entire household were baptized (Acts 16:13-15). It always amazes me that God sees an individual who is seeking for Him or desires more of God. He goes out of His way to reveal Himself through His people. The two missionaries continued with their ministry, but met with great opposition in the city, landing them in prison.

God mightily intervened on their behalf, freeing them to press on. When Paul and Silas returned from prison with wounded backs but happy hearts, they returned to Lydia's house. They could have left town immediately, but instead, they longed to encourage these new believers in their faith (Acts 16:40). Lydia was not afraid to identify with these men of God who were just severely beaten for their boldness in Christ. Though it may have caused her opposition to identify with these true disciples, she freely opened up her home. She was willing to pay the price as she had seen this same willingness modeled in Paul and Silas. Lydia also understood what Jesus had done for her. Paul and Silas met with the brothers who were gathered and encouraged them. Then they left.

We may not have to suffer beating or imprisonment as they did and as many modern-day believers endure; however, to invest in the spiritual growth of another person will cost us something. It may not be easy or come at a convenient time. It may cost us more than we planned; yet, to this God has called us and it *is* worth any kind of inconvenience or sacrifice! A thriving, loving, praying, missional, united church grew in Lydia's house despite their impossible beginning (Philippians 1:1-28). We can read a lot about them in Paul's letter to the Philippian church.

Texting, emailing, phone calls, or quick visits were not available to Paul, but the evidence of his deep love and care for them pours through the pages of his letters and prayers. He made sure to visit them, to send others on his behalf with messages and instruction for them in their new faith. The key? *Paul carried them in his heart* (Philippians 1:7).

He invested in relationships in which he deeply cared and helped them grow in Christ. This is also beautifully illustrated in the Old Testament. Whenever Aaron the priest entered God's presence in the Holy Place, he was to bear the names of every tribe, the sons of Israel, over his heart on the breastplate he wore. The names were engraved on precious stones. Thus, each time he ministered before the Lord, he remembered all the people as he carried them upon his heart (Exodus 28:15-30). What a humbling yet hopeful reminder of how Jesus, our High Priest, carries each one of us in His heart and desires to give us His heart for the people we are to reach. Imagine what would happen if every follower of Jesus would carry one or two believers in his heart, caring, encouraging, and investing, as Paul did.

Paul continued to model Christ-like living for them, even

> Imagine what would happen if every follower of Jesus would carry one or two believers in his heart, caring, encouraging, and investing, as Paul did.

in his own suffering. He wrote the Philippians, "Join together in following my example, and just as you have us as a model, keep your eyes on those who live as we do" (Philippians 3:17). Earlier in this chapter, he tells them, "not that I have already obtained all this, or have already been made perfect..." (vs. 12). Paul was still an imperfect man, but he always pointed them to Christ. Modeling is not about living in perfection but living in dependency upon Christ, pointing always to Jesus and allowing Him to work through us.

> Modeling is not about living in perfection but living in dependency upon Christ, pointing always to Jesus and allowing Him to work through us.

Teaching

Paul commended these precious new Christians in Philippi for their love, faith, and obedience, but his greatest longing was for them to know Christ Jesus intimately, to experience the closeness of His presence through personal fellowship, and to become like Him (Philippians 3:8-10).

Through Him, they would be able to discern what was best and be pure and blameless until the day of Christ (Philippians 1:9-10). He exhorted them to stand firm and to remain humble, considering others better than themselves. He reminded them to continue to work out their own salvation, but that it was God Himself who worked in them to will and to act according to His good purposes, a very important aspect to explain to new Christians (Philippians 1:27, 2:3, 2:12-13). Paul instructed the new church in the ways of the Kingdom. Some basic elements we can teach new believers as they begin their journeys are:

1. **Read God's Word every day.** Begin with the Gospel of John and read about the life of Jesus. The scriptures teach us to be *doers* of the Word and *apply* His Word to our lives.

2. **Talk with God in prayer.** God invites us to come to Him just as we are. Prayer is about spending time with Jesus and He also loves spending time with us. Prayer can include thanksgiving, repentance, petition, intercession and listening for His voice.

3. **Join a gospel centered church family.** It is essential for believers to worship together, grow, encourage each other and serve. God's Word also compels us to *be* the church in everyday life.

4. **Ask God to fill you with His Holy Spirit.** Through the Spirit we will receive boldness, wisdom, comfort and guidance to live for Christ and He empowers us to share our faith.

5. **Share the good news of Jesus.** Others need to hear our story what God has done for us, and how they can have a personal relationship with Jesus.

6. Demonstrate God's love to others. We are called to serve one another through love. Jesus did not come to be served but to serve and to lay down His life for us. We must follow in His steps.

7. Obey the command of Jesus. We can make disciples by simply showing someone how to follow Jesus as we follow Him.

Naturally, each point needs explanation and the new believers need the opportunity to encounter the ways of the kingdom as well, in order to understand their meaning. These are great conversation points that can help point someone in the right direction.

This does not mean that the same person must build the relationship, model, and teach the new believer everything he needs to know about God. A friend may model Christ through a positive relationship and bring his new believing friend to a small group. The leader may connect personally with the new believers in his group. It is vital that they connect with other believers in the family of God (Hebrews 10:25).

Do you remember Jasmine who received Christ at our Christmas love gift outreach? She posted scripture and words of encouragement on social media from time to time. Meagan, who was Jasmine's previous co-worker, saw the social media posts when her life was spiraling out of control. She reached out to Jasmine with a desperate plea for help.

This is Jasmine's story: "I interceded for God's intervention during that connection because I felt Meagan could die from drinking. I remember asking God for the next drink to make her ill because that poison should not be in her body. About an hour later, Meagan told me she poured the remaining alcohol down the drain because she got sick and felt like it would kill her. I invited Meagan to our church. Every week, I connected with her because I believed that God would do for her what He did for me. He delivered me from one moment to the next. I believed that Jesus sets the captives free and I interceded for that same transformation. Meagan came to church and God did the rest. She is an amazing woman of God."

When Meagan came to visit our church, she met Debbie. She and her husband Tom took Meagan and her son under their wing and poured their love and time into their lives to disciple them. This is Debbie's story:

"We met Meagan several years ago. What we saw when we first encountered her broke our hearts. Meagan's posture was one of shame, insecurity, fear, and hopelessness. She carried herself with her face down, hair covering her face, shoulders slumped forward, no life in her eyes. We learned that she had suffered immense abuse. She was neglected as well as physically, emotionally, and sexually abused by the very people she was supposed to be able to trust: parents, grandparents, siblings, and later, her spouse.

"Meagan went through a discipleship process by attending Live Free, as well as Sunday and Wednesday services. She also continued in a mentoring relationship with us. We just fell in love with this beautiful woman and her son. One day, Meagan called me in a very desperate place. Through wisdom from the Holy Spirit and much persuasion, I was able to get her to the church. That day, one of our pastors ministered to Meagan.

"She accepted Jesus as her Lord and Savior and chains were broken. This was the beginning of her journey to freedom! Meagan had very deep wounds that took diligent purposeful work to overcome. Her healing came as she applied herself to the Word, prayer, praise, and godly counsel.

"To look at Meg today, you would never even believe where she began. Jesus Christ has COMPLETELY transformed her life! She is free from the shame of her past. She walks with her head held high, hair back, eyes alert. She has the confidence to parent her son with love and structure. She is independent, but has the wisdom to know when she needs to reach out for help. She no longer relies on public assistance, but is able to financially provide for the needs of her family. She is an ambassador for the cause of Jesus. Meagan is a modern day living, walking, breathing testimony of the saving grace and redemptive power of the blood of Jesus Christ!!"

It is amazing how God used different people, small groups, and church services in the lives of one family. This is how the body of Christ is designed to work together, committed to make disciples for Jesus.

Even when we plant a gospel seed in a stranger we will never see again, we can entrust him into God's hand, knowing that one plants a seed, another waters, and God Himself will make it grow (1 Corinthians 3:6). He is able to bring forth much fruit from one single seed sown. Yet God is calling us to engage in the process of disciple making with those around us as we see in the life of Jesus and Paul. Just as a newborn baby needs tender loving care, so it is with a newly born-again child of God.

One Sunday, a visitor named Brian introduced Luke to me. I had never met either one of them before. Brian explained he was a traveling business man and was staying in our community for a couple of nights. He met Luke at a sporting goods store the day before and was delighted to find Luke open to the Lord. Brian wanted to make sure his newly believing friend would be discipled. He found our church online and brought Luke to one of our services, so we could follow up with him after Brian left town. We were both delighted by the fact Brian didn't only make a connection with Luke, but wanted Luke to have a church where he could be nurtured in his faith. This is in the heart of God. Don't we also see this in the story of the Good Samaritan? He did not only stop and use his resources for the half dead man, but also made the effort to bring him to the local inn and nursed him through the night. Upon leaving the wounded man in the hands of the inn keeper, the Samaritan promised to pay for whatever was needed upon his return.

When we pursue Jesus, we will love Him more deeply and become like Him!

Every new believer must grow in loving and living intimately with Jesus, embracing the truths of God's Word in a personal way so he too can make disciples (2 Timothy 2:2). Though this process takes time, sometimes it happens more easily, and other times takes a lot of patience and perseverance. The work of the Spirit is certainly needed for this transformation. "But we all, with unveiled face, beholding as in a mirror the glory of the Lord, are being transformed into the same image (His likeness) from glory to glory, just as by the Spirit of the Lord" (2 Corinthians 3:18, NKJV). Simply put, when we pursue Jesus, we will love Him more deeply and become like Him!

Mike had never known a personal relationship with Christ and his wife Michelle was Jewish. They literally went from their decisions to receive Christ directly into our New Beginnings group.

I told them they were a dream come true. Mike and Michelle were thrilled to learn more about a personal relationship with Jesus, how to study the Bible, effective prayer, love and forgiveness, water baptism, and the Holy Spirit. God was visibly at work in their lives and in their children, as well. The entire family became actively involved in the church. After some time, they became life group leaders, investing in the lives of others, and now Mike is passionately ministering to children every week, being a spiritual father to many kids.

However, discipleship does not always happen right away. One of our leaders was struggling with the slow process of a small group of women she was mentoring. She explained that when she came to Christ, she was immediately set free from drugs and alcohol and transformed by the power of God. She went to church, got involved, and never turned back. She could not understand why this was not the case for her new friends. We were able to help her recognize she was raised with biblical values such as honesty, respect, and commitment. When she was born again, she returned to the values that were previously invested in her life; however, there are people who have never learned these principles and have lived without God's standards, even for generations. When they surrender their lives to Jesus, they become a new creation as the Bible teaches.

Though every person has to learn how to grow in their new life in Christ, for some, it takes much longer as they rebuild, through the work of the Holy Spirit, what was devastated in their past (Isaiah 61:4). God is patient and longsuffering, and we must be the same.

This same desire was in Paul for the Philippian church. We also see his heart for the church in his letter to the Galatians: "My dear children, for whom I am again in the pains of childbirth until Christ is formed in you" (Galatians 4:19). To the Thessalonian Christians, Paul wrote, "But we were gentle among you, like a mother caring for her little children. We loved you so much that we were delighted to share with you not only the gospel of God, but our lives as well, because you had become so dear to us… For you know that we dealt with each of you as a father deals with his own children, encouraging, comforting and urging you to live lives worthy of God, who calls you into his kingdom and glory" (1 Thessalonians 2:7-8, 11-12). To the Corinthians, he wrote, "Even though you have ten thousand guardians in Christ, you do not have many fathers, for in Christ Jesus I became your father through the gospel. Therefore, I urge you to imitate me… Follow my example, as I follow the example of Christ" (1 Corinthians 4:15, 11:1).

When we pray for those whom God has entrusted to us, He can lead us to a specific portion of scripture or resource that would encourage or give guidance to the new believer. God is calling us to live a life in the Spirit and He will guide us. We should live in expectation of it! This is an extremely powerful way to help someone see the leading of the Spirit and it makes God's Word relevant to him.

Tracy texted a song link to her assistant Jennifer, who had recently come to Christ and was also attending our New Beginnings group with her. When Jennifer listened to the song, she was amazed. It contained the exact same meaning as the scripture she had just finished reading several times. The timing was perfect; it made God real and the Bible relevant. She was excited, anticipating more discoveries in the Word of God.

My sister sent me a link on my phone to a short prayer done by her son-in-law. Within seconds, I forwarded this powerful prayer to a few new believers. They all responded within minutes how timely this prayer was. What a difference even one text, call, or visit, led by His Spirit, can make in the life of a new believer who is in the process of becoming a true disciple of Jesus Christ!

We befriended our neighbors across the street, Mark and Leigh Ann, and enjoyed getting to know them. Eventually, Leigh Ann came to visit our church, knowing we were very involved with our church family. She and her two children committed their lives to Christ and we rejoiced together. We then started meeting with her and another neighbor for a few weeks to discuss the basics of our faith. We went through a small book together, discussing any questions that came up and praying together. She then joined our church and other small groups with people in our church. Eventually, Leigh Ann went with us on one of our foreign missions trips to Romania and shared the love of God with children. We continued to agree together in prayer for her husband and God answered our prayers. At first, he came to support his wife and children who were involved in our Christmas production. However, before this dear family moved away from our community, Mark decided to become a follower of Jesus, as well. Though we hated to see them leave, the entire family is still faithfully serving God and they are connected with another church family in their new town. Leigh Ann recently told me, "The connections we made still exist seven years after our family moved from the area... connections that make us feel as if Calvary's Love will always be a place to call 'home.'"

Though I wish true discipleship would always happen automatically in the family of God, it doesn't always work out that way. I have observed that it becomes more natural the more we do it. Church leaders can also help facilitate this by helping a new believer connect with someone more mature in the faith.

Shirley is a retired woman and a devoted follower of Jesus. Some time ago, we asked her if she would be able to disciple a precious single mom, who was struggling in her walk with Christ. We knew it would make a difference if she had someone who could personally be connected with her and who could encourage her along the way. Shirley eagerly accepted and said it was an answer to prayer. She had just been praying that God would open a door to be used by Him. Shirley took her assignment from God seriously and began calling, texting, and meeting with her new friend regularly. By showing interest in her life, providing accountability, and encouraging her in Christ, Shirley is persistent to help this precious woman to receive the help she desperately needs and overcome her struggles to be victorious! As a result, this single mom has discovered her true value in Christ. Shirley has come along side many other women, helping them grow in Christ.

We also encourage our prayer team that prays with individuals receiving Christ during church services or events to make sure they call or connect with the new believers afterward.

Who has God placed in your life in need of encouragement today? Is there someone you haven't seen lately at church and you can take a moment to give them a call or visit them? It is Christ's heart to go after the *missing* (Ezekiel 34:16, Luke 15:3-7). Is there a small group or special event in your church to which you could invite a new believer? Who is God calling you to share a relationship with and help him grow in Jesus? I want to encourage you to answer the call of Jesus to make disciples. Those whom He calls, He also equips.

"The One who calls you is faithful, and He will do it" (1 Thessalonians 5:24).

REFLECTION AND APPLICATION

1. What speaks to you from the example of Jesus and Paul concerning discipleship?

2. Is there someone you connected with, perhaps you planted a seed or led someone to Christ, who needs follow-up? Is there someone you know who is missing from your church family? What can you do to reconnect him/her?

3. Follow-up should always lead to discipleship. What does discipleship mean to you?

4. Is there someone God is asking you to disciple? What are some things you can do to personally help them grow as a believer?

5. Why is relationship such an integral part of being a disciple? What benefits are gained through being relational with a new believer?

6. What does modeling the Christian life look like to you?

7. Did someone walk alongside you when you accepted Jesus? What effect did that have on your walk with Christ?

8. Why are prayer and patience both necessary components to discipleship? Is there someone God is asking you to have more patience with in their walk with Christ? In what ways have you grown as the direct result of the prayers or patience of another?

9. What steps will you take to disciple a new believer?

9

THE NATIONS

"Therefore go and make disciples of *all* nations, baptizing them in the name of the Father and of the Son and of the Holy Spirit, and teaching them to obey *everything* I have commanded you. And surely I am with you *always*, to the very end of the age" (Matthew 28:19-20). With these words, Jesus commissioned His disciples just before ascending to heaven.

What did Jesus mean by "*all* nations"? Is this commission just for a chosen few who are missionaries in other nations? Do these scriptures imply we must reach people beyond our own community? If Jesus directed this commission to *every* believer, how would this be possible?

The word commission means: The act of granting certain powers or the authority to carry out a particular task or duty. The task authorized. As representatives of Jesus, we are commissioned, or authorized, by Him to carry out the specific task given to us. Christ gave this commission to *all* of His followers of *every* generation.

Many of us see our own community but maybe not far beyond it. We are definitely called to reach the lost and the broken in our communities, but we also need to recognize the Father's heart for the *nations*. The world was in God's heart from the very beginning. When God loved, He loved the *world*. His Son died for the *world*. Jesus said, "Go into *all* the world and preach the good news to *all* creation" (Mark 16:15).

God hears the cries of the world, and when we draw near to Him, we will hear them, too. Do you hear the cry of the children living on the streets, the women who are abused, those in foreign lands who exhaust themselves in effort to find forgiveness and hope? Do you hear the cry of the rich, the religious, and those who have turned to everything else besides Jesus? There is also the cry from the skeptics, the post-moderns, those asking the difficult questions. God hears the cry of their souls for the truth though many don't know that is what they are seeking. And God is looking for those whom He can send. In Isaiah's encounter with God's presence, he heard the voice of the Lord saying, "Whom shall I send? And who will go for us?" Isaiah promptly responded, "Here am I, send me." And God commanded, "Go" (Isaiah 6:8-9).

Some people ask, "Why should I go somewhere else when there is still so much work to be done at home?" Jesus said the mission field is the *world* (Matthew 13:38). He also said, "...Open your eyes and look at the *fields!* They are ripe for harvest" (John 4:35). The mission field is not just the country in which we live. It is the *entire* world.

Mark 1:33-38 tells the story of the town of Capernaum that had gathered at the door where Jesus was. He healed many of various diseases and drove out many demons. Very early the next morning, the disciples found Jesus praying in a solitary place. They exclaimed, "Everyone is looking for you." I'm sure the people were waiting to hear Him teach, preach, and heal again. To their surprise, He replied, "Let us go somewhere else, to the nearby villages, so I can preach there also. That is why I have come." He left the crowd behind and traveled on to another place.

> Jesus said the mission field is the *world*. He also said, "Open your eyes and look at the fields! They are ripe for harvest."

There are men and women who are specifically called to go to a certain nation. Growing up in the Netherlands as a ten-year-old girl, I remember telling a family friend, "When I finish school, I am going to America." This desire to go never left me. As I grew up, I thought it meant that I would go just for a year's visit to work in church ministry and learn the English language.

I did not realize at the time it was a calling for life. I have many family members and friends who are serving God in a specific nation in response to God's calling. Others are based in their homeland and travel abroad to minister in various ways through preaching, teaching, church planting, training, and children's and youth work. Yet how can each one of us fulfill this great commission? How can *we* make disciples of all nations?

Pray

Isn't it easy to be consumed with the prayer burdens of our own lives, our church, and our community with little or no energy left to pray for others around the world? God's heart is for *every* person to know Him. He invites us to be participants with Him to pray and proclaim His name among the nations, tribes, and unreached people groups, those who have never once heard about the name of Jesus. When our hearts are open before God, He pours His heart into ours by His Spirit. When we pray specifically for the people of other nations, the burden and compassion for the world will increase.

Jesus said, "*My* house will be called a house of prayer for all nations" (Mark 11:17). I want to be part of "*His* House." God calls for His church to rise both individually as well as corporately and take her position to fervently pray in light of worsening conditions in our world today. When church leaders include praying for a specific country during their worship service, it helps believers to be aware of the needs of people in other nations.

> "The heartfelt and persistent prayer of a righteous man (believer) can accomplish much (when put into action and made effective by God—it is dynamic and can have tremendous power)" (James 5:16, AMP).

As I left for our weekly Tuesday morning prayer group, I turned some music on in my car. The words of a song were ringing in my heart, "In the name of Jesus is salvation, healing, and deliverance." I started to declare His power in the name of Jesus for the salvation of the lost among the nations. Suddenly, the Holy Spirit came over me and I started laughing out loud in victory. I just could not stop and had such an amazing breakthrough in prayer. I was convinced in that moment that though the world groans under the effects of sin, God is still building His kingdom through His people, His church. "... I will build My church, and the gates of hell shall not prevail against it" (Matthew 16:18, KJV). I arrived at our church with great anticipation; however, several of the ladies were burdened with personal challenges and needs. One lady's son had just been incarcerated. Sharing in her pain, we prayed with her. I also explained about my personal breakthrough that morning and what God had shown me about the nations.

> I was convinced in that moment that though the world groans under the effects of sin, God is still building His kingdom through His people, His church.

As a result, the lady whose son was incarcerated began to pray from the depths of her heart for this generation. Through her own anguish, she felt how God's heart was broken over the nations, yearning for them to be saved. The Holy Spirit ignited the entire group to pray fervently despite the difficult situations they were facing, and we all experienced a strong presence of the Lord. We knew God was hearing our prayers. "Ask of Me, and I will give You the nations for Your inheritance, And the ends of the earth for Your possession" (Psalm 2:8 NKJV).

It is still "our time" and God-given privilege and responsibility to push back the darkness. "For the secret power of lawlessness is already at work; but the one who now holds it back will continue to do so till He is taken out of the way" (2 Thessalonians 2:7).

I pray that faith by God's Spirit will rise up in you at this very moment with this realization. I pray that a passion and Holy Spirit-fueled determination to build God's holy nation and kingdom will ignite you to pray and go make disciples in His name!

God can move a nation in response to the prayers of one man (i.e., Daniel), but when believers come together in united prayer, the effects multiply. A team from our church went on a prayer and evangelism missions trip to work with missionaries Rich and Jenni Demartino, who were planting a new church in Guadalajara, Mexico. We prayed fervently God would open the hearts of the Mexican people we were to reach. Each day, we prayed that the Holy Spirit would lead us before going into the community, and as a result, the Spirit led us to connect with specific people. These were such powerful times of prayer.

As our team was walking in downtown Guadalajara, Julia, a team member, suddenly began to weep uncontrollably. I stopped to see what had happened. Had she fallen or was she hurting? She explained that she had seen a man sitting on the street at the gate of a cathedral and that God's Spirit was moving her deeply with compassion for this man. Our missionary Jenni and I walked back with Julia to speak to the man. I had walked by the same place and had not noticed him. How easy it is to overlook those we meet along the way. We found out his name was Juan and he looked pitiful indeed, slumped on the ground, eyes half closed, and leaning against the gate with an empty liquor bottle next to him. We told him that Jesus loved him and wanted to set him free. Julia shared her personal story of how God had delivered her from drugs and alcohol. He looked right at us and seemed very interested. I was wondering if God did a miracle by giving him a clear mind at that very moment. We went through the Jesus story with him and Juan was ready to give his life to Jesus. I will never ever forget the moment when he looked up at us with a big smile. Juan encountered Jesus and was deeply moved. He thanked us for stopping and appreciated the food we gave him. The Holy Spirit helped Julia to see this treasure the way God sees him. Unspeakable joy flooded our hearts as God shares the joy in heaven with those who participate with Him in leading someone to Christ.

Manuel, our taxi driver, was munching on a bag of chips as he was driving us back to our hotel from downtown Guadalajara. His eyes looked empty and lifeless. All I could think was, "This man looks so dead." We asked him some questions and he answered without any expression. Manuel told us that he had been a taxi driver for fifteen years and that he was going through a divorce. The Holy Spirit prompted us to explain that true happiness and fulfillment for the void in our lives cannot be expected to come from our spouse or any other person. It is only found in Jesus Christ by knowing Him in personal relationship. This brought our conversation with this searching man to the things of God. Manuel told us that he had asked God if He was real to show Himself, but that God had not answered his prayers. We were thrilled to tell him that God had just done this by putting us in his car. Some of the team members had even requested to stop for five minutes to look inside a cathedral, but instead, we had left right away with the taxies. God knew we needed to be in this particular car with this chosen treasure. We wanted him to recognize how much God loved him, saw him, and heard his prayer. When we asked him if he would like to receive Jesus into his life, he responded that he first had to work on himself because he was ashamed of his life. He confided in us that he had hurt a lot of people and spent several years in prison. Andy, one of our team members, shared his story of how God had delivered him from drugs and alcohol. Michelle, who was also with us, told her story of how God had forgiven her from having an abortion. As we arrived at the hotel, we asked if we could show him the story of Jesus through the evangycube (a multi-panel cube that tells the story of the gospel of Christ in pictures).

There on the busy street, with the door open, we had the opportunity to tell Manuel the Jesus story illustrated with pictures. We felt he was moved by the story and understood it. When we asked if he was ready to receive the Savior, we were surprised with his response, "This is not the moment." We thanked him and explained he could ask to receive Jesus whenever he was ready. As he drove away, we were disappointed, but we knew a powerful seed was planted. We all joined hands and prayed that Manuel would come to know Jesus in a personal way. The next day, Jenni met me with a big smile on her face. "Guess who called? Manuel, the taxi driver! He told me that after he dropped you off, he picked up another group of people who also were born again Christians and also witnessed to him! He said to himself, 'This cannot be an accident,' and as he thought this, he saw a vision of Jesus in heaven." This all impacted him and therefore he wanted to come to church that night to give his life to Jesus.

The team and I rejoiced and cried at the same time. We thanked God for His faithfulness. When Manuel walked into the church that night, we all cheered! I do not know if this was embarrassing to him, but he could tell we all genuinely cared and rejoiced with him, which was hard for him to understand. Manuel was gloriously born again as he repented from his sin and received Jesus as his Lord and Savior. Truly, he once was dead and is now alive! His eyes were radiant, his face filled with life and hope. Manuel did not even look like the same person. As he said goodbye to go back to work, he expressed deep gratitude to the team and was surprised about the joy and peace he felt. We told him, we were the grateful ones, as it is such a privilege and joy to see a life literally transformed by the love of the Father! Together with the team, we discussed the seven-seed principle which we discussed in chapter three. An initial rejection does not always mean a final decision. In Manuel's situation, we were the sixth seed and the people he picked up after us were the seventh seed, which led to his readiness to be born again!

We were praising God for mightily answering our prayers and the powerful services in the new church. These precious people were hungry to receive from God. We were thankful to have a small part and continue to believe the Lord of the harvest for His mighty work!

Missionaries, the church around the world, and the persecuted church are in urgent need of our prayer support, as well. They *depend* on our prayers! When I read about our persecuted brothers and sisters, I am quickly reminded of the great hardships these steadfast believers face, which is an everyday reality. In many restricted nations, being a Christian or sharing Christ can lead to great suffering, even imprisonment and death. Their courageous testimonies inspire me to pray for them and live more boldly for Christ. Missionaries have shared countless miracles about bringing the word of life to the unreached. God opened doors, provided funds, and protected lives as an individual or the church moved the hand of God through prayer. We will not realize the full impact of our prayers until heaven, but be assured, they are bearing fruit around the world.

Tammy awoke at 3:30 a.m. with an urgency from the Holy Spirit to pray for my daughter Rachelle, who is serving in Romania as a missionary. The next day Tammy, who lives in Pennsylvania, contacted Rachelle through email to inform her about her prayer burden and to ask her if she was okay. Upon reading the email, Rachelle began to weep, knowing God was revealing His love to her. At exactly the time Tammy was praying, Rachelle was dealing with a devastating situation, heavy with discouragement. After that obedient prayer, God worked a complete miracle and restored the entire situation. Prayer knows no distance!

Jesus said, "The harvest is plentiful but the workers are few. Ask (pray) the Lord of the harvest, therefore, to send out workers into His harvest field" (Matthew 9:37). About 5.3 billion people around the world are still waiting to receive the good news of Jesus. Many more workers are needed for the desperate need of the unreached. It is therefore

> He is pleased but also obligated to answer this prayer since He Himself told us to pray this prayer.

important to pray God will raise up workers for His harvest field. I have heard it said that He is pleased but also obligated to answer this prayer since He Himself told us to pray this prayer.

Regardless of what our participation in missions looks like, we can all begin with prayer. From this place, a deeper conviction of God's desire to reach the world will grow in us and compel us to join Him in His great work, which is a great privilege.

Give

> "How then, can they call on the One they have not believed in? And how can they believe in the One of whom they have not heard? And how can they hear without someone preaching to them? *And how can they preach unless they are sent?* As it is written: 'How beautiful are the feet of those who bring good news'" (Romans 10:14-15).

We know generosity makes a difference. Yet we do not always realize the impact the gospel can have in the world through our giving. We are either called to go or to send a substitute, but we all must do our part. If we cannot go, then we must help send those who preach the gospel and support those who do the work of God in other nations. There are many people who have caught the vision to help someone else go or donate financial support needed for mission projects.

Paul thanked the Philippian church for their generous support: "...Not one church shared with me in the matter of giving... except you only... you sent me aid again and again when I was in need...

[these gifts] are a fragrant offering, an acceptable sacrifice, pleasing to God. And my God will meet all your needs according to His glorious riches in Christ Jesus" (Philippians 4:15-16, 18-19).

Through their faithful giving, Paul was able to go, witness, and plant churches in Europe and Asia. I am sure they did not realize that at times, they were the only support to the work of the Lord through Paul. Through our giving and praying, we will share in the blessing and reward of the harvest. Even when you feel you do not have much to give, you can pray for God to provide the seed you desire to sow and trust that He will multiply it as you give.

> Even when you feel you do not have much to give, you can pray for God to provide the seed you desire to sow and trust that He will multiply it as you give.

"Now he who *supplies* seed to the sower and bread for food will also supply and *increase* your store of seed and will enlarge the harvest of your righteousness. You will be made rich in every way so that you can be generous on every occasion, and through us your generosity will result in thanksgiving to God" (2 Corinthians 9:10-11).

A small church in a rural area of upstate New York decided to invest in missions through their summer Vacation Bible School event. All week, the leaders shared about the needs of orphans in

Romania with the children and families. They caught the vision and excitedly began raising funds totaling $200 by the end of the week. Upon receiving the funds, Rachelle and her team set out to buy much needed clothing and shoes for seventeen orphaned children in a state center of Bucharest. They were excited for the opportunity to share the love of Jesus with these precious children and meet some practical needs. As Diana, one of the team members, shared what she was doing with a friend, the mission grew. Diana's friend owns a clothing company and wanted to get in on the mission! She decided to donate clothing and shoes for all the children at the center, enabling the missions team to use the $200 for another group of orphans at another center! God tripled the $200 offering from this church in New York to bless more children in need. When we give what we have, God will increase and multiply it to go much further than we imagined (Mark 6:30-44).

The church has the privilege and opportunity to support missionaries and missions' efforts around the world. It is our joy to assist in purchasing Bibles in the language of the receiver, provide much needed resources and equipment for churches or compassion efforts, provide a means of transportation for a missionary, and help build churches and Bible schools.

We also have wide-open opportunities to provide basic needs such as food, blankets, and clean water to families in villages who have never had clean water or to those who have suffered disasters. This makes a way to bring the love of Jesus to those who are suffering and hurting. "The King will say to those on his right, 'Come, you who are blessed by my Father; take your inheritance, the kingdom prepared for you since the creation of the world. For I was hungry and you gave me something to eat, I was thirsty and you gave me something to drink, I was a stranger and you invited me in, I needed clothes and you clothed me, I was sick and you looked after me, I was in prison and you came to visit me'" (Matthew 25:34-36).

Years ago, I watched a father starve to death in Africa as he gave his last piece of bread to his wife and two children. I was weeping, tears streaming down my face, seeing the sad scene unfold in front of me on the television screen. The Holy Spirit spoke to my heart: "Esther, people all around you are *spiritually* starving to death and you must give them the bread of life." This experience greatly impacted my life. It is a privilege that God has called us to bring Jesus, the bread of life, to those nearby and faraway.

It is not just the giving of our finances that can make a difference, but also giving of our time and abilities. Teri, a mom of four with a passion for missions, has gone several times on mission trips with our church; however, since she couldn't always go, she used her gift of administration and organization to help prepare the teams for these trips. This is an indispensable gift that builds God's kingdom in other nations. Teri told me, "Serving in missions isn't just something I do. It's part of who I am, who God designed me to be."

Lauren, another woman told me, "I really enjoy helping the teams prepare the music, dramas, and other things they need for their mission. It is one way I can invest in missions even when I cannot go myself."

In essence, giving of your time and talents in your local church can indirectly affect the nations, as well. I think of the teacher in kids' church giving opportunity for children to learn about Jesus and His heart for the world. In God's presence, right here in kids' church, several children were called to missions. I think of the elderly usher who stopped a woman leaving the church and gently offered to pray for her. As a result, she was saved that day and later became a missionary to India. How about two faithful men in our church, who have annually sponsored many children to attend kids' camp?

As a result, many children have had encounters with Jesus in powerful camp services, dedicating their lives to Him and are now serving in the place of their calling. A woman in our church took a part-time job one summer for the purpose of using that income for outreach and missions. She offered to help sponsor someone to go on a missions trip our church was taking that year. Unknown to her, a single mom and a single dad had each taken a step of faith to sign up for the trip, sensing God was leading them to do so, but lacked any funds to pay for the trip. When she discovered their need, she was overjoyed that God answered her prayer and was excited to cover the cost of both.

God asks all of His children to put *first* His kingdom and His righteousness (Matthew 6:33). The thought of putting first His kingdom can mean different things to us. It helps me to remember all I am and everything I have belongs to God. In other words, our time, talents, and treasures belong to Him and we hold them loosely in our hands. It is a privilege He has made us stewards over all He has entrusted to us (1 Corinthians 4:2). When we come to Jesus daily, praying

> Our time, talents, and treasures belong to Him and we hold them loosely in our hands.

and believing for His Kingdom and His will to be done in our lives, He will always guide us. Jesus says: "Do not store up for yourselves treasures on earth, where moth and rust destroy, and where thieves break in and steal. But store up for yourselves treasures in heaven, where moth and rust do not destroy, and where thieves do not break in and steal. For where your treasure is, there your heart will be also" (Matthew 6:19-21). Jesus was teaching us to live our lives in the *light of eternity!*

The ideas for missions are inexhaustible. You can contact your pastor for missions giving opportunities.

Go

Foreign missions trips have ignited a passion in our church family for reaching our world. Through these short-term missions trips, several team members have received a call to become career missionaries. Others have received a call to children's ministry, youth ministry, prison ministry, or simply been ignited to live on mission with God in everyday life.

My husband Jerry recounts the unforgettable times when he visited Ecuador. His first trips to Ecuador with teams from our church were filled with outreach ministry to adults and children in villages, to support and serve a new church plant that was meeting in a tent. They also helped build the foundations of the new church facility. He joined our host missionaries, Tim and Debbie Anderson, and many Ecuadorians in a heartfelt prayer of dedication as they opened their new church facility called Calvary's Love. This church building is located in an isolated village and stands as a strong lighthouse for the glory of God! Since then, this church has planted three additional churches in other towns. Many adults and children received Christ during these services and others were healed and set free by the mighty power of God. A distraught mom brought her sick baby to the tent service and God healed the baby miraculously! Others who came in discouraged and depressed were set free when they experienced an outpouring of the Holy Spirit. The pastors and church members were greatly encouraged by all that took place through the power of God!

Steve grew up in our church and was first called to the nations as a teenager while going on a missions trip to South America. Since then, God has called Steve and his wife Jill as missionaries to Uruguay. My husband Jerry led a team from our church to Uruguay to work with our host missionaries. God did an amazing miracle while they were there.

This is Steve's story:

"We did not know that Juan and Daniela were witchdoctors and the head sorcerers of the local satanic cult when they gave us permission to use their land. The plan was for the team from my home church in New York to kick off children's outreaches, with the hope of planting a new church in this community. We began to pray for their salvation and believe God to do a miracle in their lives.

"While our team was ministering to the children, God started a work in the lives of Juan and Daniela. Juan began to sense God's presence as he watched us from his window and was impacted as he heard the songs, Bible stories, and prayer during the children's outreaches. It is amazing how the power of God can start to work, even while watching from a distance."

This is Juan's story:

"I got up early the next morning after the team left and looked in my back yard. It immediately struck me that the lawn was covered with beautiful white flowers. I scanned my neighbors' yards all around and couldn't find any other place that had white flowers, except in the place where the children had been praying, singing worship songs, and learning about Jesus. I tried to step out of my back door, and immediately, I felt overwhelmed with the presence and love of God. I fell on my knees right then and said, 'Your God is more powerful than mine and I want to serve Him.'"

Shortly after our team returned home, we received the news that Juan and Daniela showed up at church with their ritual robes and books full of incantations and spells. They placed their faith in God and were set free in a powerful way. They burned all their books and ritual clothes and were water baptized. This precious couple love the Lord and faithfully attend the church. While part of the satanic cult, Juan and Danielle had lost their infant son, but God has blessed them with a second son. His name is Emanuel: "God is with us." Since then, Juan and Daniela have had an incredible impact on their community as their conversion has led many others to move away from satanic cult and join the church.

Many people in our church have used their time and talents to build God's kingdom in another part of the Father's harvest field, knowing people are joining the kingdom and being transformed. At times, people from other churches have joined our team on a missions trip when their church was not able to organize a trip themselves. It is effective when churches work together in missions.

Throughout my childhood, my father served as a pastor and evangelist, often traveling to other countries to bring the gospel of Jesus Christ. Through the years, we have seen abundant fruit from his ministry. God showed my parents that this was not just his calling but a family calling. My mother took the mantle of prayer in this ministry. God showed her that through prayer, she would be with him and share in the harvest. She participated through prayer and provided a stability for her children at home. That was her part. Because of their perspective, they sowed a kingdom perspective in our family. These positive seeds are now bearing fruit in their children and grandchildren, many of whom are participating in missions and obeying God's call to the nations. When a family or a church sees missions as their calling, they will all participate in reaching the nations, and together, we will *all* do our part.

Whether we are in our own land or on a foreign field, God has called us to live on mission with Him. Every believer is called to go into his world of influence and beyond, to shine the light of Jesus.

Many people from other nations have come to us. This gives us another opportunity to reach them. Myriam was called to be a missionary as a young girl. She wondered what this exactly would look like. Throughout her teenage years and early adulthood, she had a desire to live abroad and teach foreign languages. She never dreamed God was calling her as a missionary to foreign exchange students here in her own community. Myriam works as an English as a Second Language teacher for foreign students at a university in our town. God is at work in these students and Myriam never ceases to be amazed by the work of the Holy Spirit.

I will never forget Myriam's text message informing me she was bringing three foreign students to our New Beginnings group for new believers one Wednesday. She told me that one was an atheist from East Germany, another a Buddhist student from Taiwan, and another a German student who did not have a relationship with Christ. We were thrilled to have them, but not sure how they would respond. The students were receptive and kind. They continued to attend after the first week, each time hearing more about Jesus.

They had many questions and we met with them a few times individually, explaining God's plan of salvation and discussing their questions. They had never heard these truths before. It was rewarding to experience their openness and hunger for God. When we discussed the lesson about the love of God and forgiveness, we explained the way of salvation through Jesus Christ and His death on the cross. God's love was drawing these students and they each responded to join God's family and give their lives to Jesus! The Buddhist student started crying, explaining she had never experienced this before and didn't know why she was crying. It was a marvelous night. They came every time the church doors were open. Before returning back to their countries, we were able to give them a study Bible and some other helpful study materials. Their departure was bittersweet, as we hated to say goodbye, but we were beyond grateful they had found Christ. Now they were going back to their homelands to let their light shine. Myriam has remained connected with them through email and phone since they left, encouraging them in their relationship with Christ.

Myriam invited a couple to our church from the Middle East who are also studying at our university. They heard the gospel of Jesus for the very first time. Both were moved in their hearts by

God's love to receive Christ and participated in our New Beginnings group. We shared in their joy as they publicly declared their faith in Jesus and followed Him in obedience to be water baptized! This was the wife's testimony: "The first time I came to this church, I felt strange. I remember listening to the songs and looking at the cross on the wall. It was then that I felt crucified with His love for me. I felt His love for me and it sunk deep into my heart. From that day on, I felt urged to re-enter and to my own surprise, I had the desire to know more about Jesus Christ and to be baptized." This precious couple continues to learn more about Jesus who saved them.

At times, you may feel somewhat intimidated by people from other nations, afraid you may not understand them; however, most of them are open to connect and find a place to belong. The influx of foreign students and families coming to the United States is providing us with amazing opportunities to share the gospel with people. Many of them come from countries where believers are forbidden to share the gospel. Is there a foreign student you can reach or befriend? Is there someone from another culture or country to whom you can show the love of Jesus?

Is there someone from another culture or country to whom you can show the love of Jesus?

Sometimes people travel to other nations for business or family visits. Why not pray for an opportunity to plant a seed while you are on the way or in the country itself? On our way to Budapest, Hungary, from Romania, where our daughter and her husband serve, we drove through many Hungarian villages. I softly whispered a prayer: "Lord, do the people here know You? Is there any witness for the Lord in these villages? Any church? Has anyone ever come to tell them about Jesus?" As I prayed, a strong desire overwhelmed my heart to tell these people about the love of Jesus. I asked the Lord to enable me to plant a seed in Hungary before I left. As we went through our day, I looked for potential opportunities.

We spent a night in Budapest and, to my disappointment, I had not made any significant connection. I wondered if the seed would be planted with our hotel personnel since Jerry had several conversations with them. They also spoke English very well, which was a great help! As we checked out, God opened the door to speak to them about Jesus. Their hearts were open, and they gladly took the testimony DVD we gave them. As I walked away, I noticed the girl I had a short connection with the previous day in the restaurant. I was able to tell her how God connected us again for a reason and how much He loved her. She wanted to exchange emails, and with tears in her eyes, she accepted my DVD testimony gift. I could not believe God made this happen at the last moment. He answered my prayer to sow a seed in Hungary in the short time I was there. Since then, I was thrilled to learn that there is a growing, thriving church in Budapest and though the national church in other towns is healthy, they are believing God for greater fruit and more workers to join them in the harvest field of Hungary. Currently, I love sending people a link to a specific message or point them to a certain website.

Leaving Budapest, we were seated next to a woman on the airplane to the Netherlands. Tired from a busy day, we were both enjoying some reading. Later during the flight, we got into a conversation with Janina, the lady next to us. She inquired about the book I was reading. I told her it was called *The Pastor's Wife* by Sabina Wurmbrand. It is the true story of the wife of Richard Wurmbrand, pastor and martyr during Romania's communist years.

Janina expressed her surprise because she was born and raised in Lithuania. She was able to relate with the challenges of that time. The book gave us such common ground for discussion, and she could not believe she "happened" to sit next to us. She told us that she was working in The Hague, Netherlands, for the government. We were on our way to the exact same city and realized we would be ministering in The Hague that Sunday morning where my brother, David, is the pastor. When we invited Janina to join us for the church service that Sunday morning, she gladly accepted. We were excited that Janina indeed kept her word and came the following morning for the service! She had never been in a life-giving church. During the worship, Janina kept commenting on how moving the service was. When Pastor David offered prayer for those who had specific needs, tears were streaming down her face. "I feel such a warm presence," she told me. The Holy Spirit was doing His work in this beautiful woman. We had lunch together afterward and encouraged her in a personal relationship with Jesus.

What is your part in making disciples of all nations? Is God stirring your heart to go on a missions trip or to go as a missionary for a longer period of time? Are you sending others through your financial support of missions for the gospel of the kingdom to be preached? Are you praying for those who are on the frontlines of the battle and praying for open doors? If God called you to live in another country, would you be willing to go? If He called a family member, would you be willing to let them go?

When our daughter Rachelle was about seven years old, God gave me a dream that she was on the missions field ministering to children. I did not know exactly what it meant, but kept it in my heart. Since then, God gave her a call for missions and she went on various missions trips. When she expressed her desire and calling to go to Romania, we were not surprised. She went for one year to minister to many children in this beautiful Eastern European country. She is now ministering full time together with her husband, Ruben, reaching many students and families in Bucharest, Romania.

When I struggled at first to let my daughter go, I repeatedly prayed that God would help me to obey Him from my heart. In His mercy, He showed me that by letting her go, I would share in preparing the inheritance of the nations, which the Father has promised His Son as a reward for His sacrifice. This is a great privilege! He then filled my heart with joy and a greater love for the nations.

God keeps pointing out 1 Peter 2:9, concerning the younger generation, that He has chosen them (*this generation*) to be His priesthood and holy nation, a people belonging solely to Him to declare His praises to those who are near and far. They are the ones who are looking for a worthy cause for which to spend their lives, no matter the cost.

I recognize the Spirit moving and orchestrating the passing of the baton to those of you in this next generation. The cry of my heart to you is this: "Recognize what God is doing and hear what the Spirit is saying. He is inviting you to join Him in His great work. Open your eyes and see that the harvest is ready." I also have a heart cry to those of you in my generation for our place in this process, as well. We are called to pursue God wholeheartedly, praying *fervently* for this next generation, and to live the life of Christ passionately before them, so that they can see what it looks like to "come and go"!

Yes, in the midst of darkness, He *is* building *His* church, a priesthood of faithful believers, who love Him with all their hearts and carry the Spirit and presence of Jesus. They *are* answering His call, "Whom shall I send? And who will go for us?" with a brave, "Yes, Lord, send me!" There is nothing God cannot do with a life that is fully surrendered to Him!

> In the midst of darkness, He *is* building *His* church, a priesthood of faithful believers, who love Him with all their hearts and carry the Spirit and presence of Jesus.

Live Dead

Live Dead is a missionary, church planting movement of the Assemblies of God. Hundreds of courageous young men and women who are part of the Live Dead movement are fully committing to abide in Christ and surrender their lives to obey God's will and the great commission of Christ whatever the cost. They are committed to plant churches among unreached people groups.

> There is nothing God cannot do with a life that is fully surrendered to Him!

A member of the Live Dead team in North Africa writes:

"Live Dead is a call to radical love for Jesus and sacrificial love for the world. Live Dead is a call to announce the life of God among the perishing. Live Dead is an admission that in order to reach the lost, there is much of our flesh that must die so the life of God might be manifested in our mortal bodies. We die that Christ lives in us. We die that others may live."

Bishop Phillips Brooks from the Live Dead journal challenges us all:

"Do not pray for easy lives; pray to be stronger men. Do not pray for tasks equal to your powers. Pray for powers equal to your tasks. Then the doing of your work shall be no miracle. But you shall be a miracle."[6]

The world is changing, and we are quickly running out of time. It is His command and therefore our calling to go into all the world and preach the good news to all creation and to make disciples of all nations. If you sense God stirring your heart, seek to do your part, and He will lead you. *His command is our calling!*

For more information concerning the Live Dead church-planting teams among unreached peoples, contact www.Live-Dead.org

"The concern for world evangelization is not something tacked on to a man's personal Christianity, which he may take or leave as he chooses. It is rooted in the character of God who has come to us in Christ Jesus. Thus, it can never be the province of a few enthusiasts, a sideline or a specialty of those who happen to have a bent that way. It is the distinctive mark of being a Christian" (James S. Stewart)

REFLECTION AND APPLICATION

1. What speaks to you from the example of Jesus in Mark 1:33-38?

2. What does the "great commission" mean to you?

3. Explain the importance the role of prayer plays in reaching the nations. What benefits or fruit can we expect to see through these prayers?

4. Have you developed a time of prayer for the nations? If not, what is hindering you from doing so? How can you overcome this obstacle?

5. Everything we are and everything we have ultimately belongs to Christ. In what ways does this biblical truth inspire you to be generous for His Kingdom?

6. Do you know of someone who is from another culture or nation that you can reach out to? What are some other ways you can personally be a part of spreading the gospel to other nations?

7. Have you ever gone on a missions trip into a foreign nation? If yes, what did God do in and through you during that time? If you've never gone on a missions trip, do you feel the Lord stirring your heart to do so? What are you willing to do to fulfill this call? Is there anything holding you back or intimidating you from going?

8. What steps will you take this week to be a part of the "great commission"?

THE PERSEVERANCE

Delays in prayer are not denials.

Some years ago, my friend Debbie told me, "I'm waiting on God, whenever He is ready." She was referring to a much-needed change in her husband's life. To that I responded, "Maybe God is patiently waiting on your husband instead and you are waiting together with the Lord." Isaiah 30:18 says, "Therefore the Lord will wait, that He may be gracious to you; and therefore, He will be exalted, that He may have mercy on you. For the Lord is a God of justice; blessed are all those who wait for Him" (NKJV).

God is patiently working and waiting for the fruit of the harvest. "The Lord is not slow in keeping His promise, as some understand slowness. He is patient with you, not wanting anyone to perish, but everyone to come to repentance" (2 Peter 3:9). Waiting is never wasted. God uses the season of delay to prepare us and those around us so that we will be ready for His kingdom purpose to propel us into our destiny. "… An instrument … made holy, useful to the Master and prepared to do any good work" (2 Timothy 2:21).

> God uses the season of delay to prepare us and those around us so that we will be ready for His kingdom purpose to propel us into our destiny.

Debbie's husband Tom has since completely surrendered his life to Jesus Christ and has been set free from alcoholism. She told me, "I do not recognize my own husband. He has been completely transformed. God has answered my prayer and has done an amazing work!" Tom and Debbie now minister together with great compassion to disciple others as small group leaders and serve on our 'Live Free' leadership team.

Persevering prayer is powerful, vital, and life changing. Persevering prayer for lost souls is faithfully approaching God on their behalf and *interceding* for their personal salvation. Jesus Christ is personally interceding for us in heaven and is looking for those who are willing to join Him in standing "in the gap" on behalf of the lost (Ezekiel 22:30). It is absolutely God's will and calling for believers to engage in such faith-filled prayer for unbelievers. Though the road might be difficult, it will become a "journey with God" for your own life if you continue in perseverance. God will use it to bring you closer to Him and teach you more about this walk of faith. The lessons you learn on this journey are priceless! Sometimes we break strongholds in the name of Jesus, declaring God's promises, while other times we simply rest in faith. I will always remember the time God gave me the scripture, "…having done all, to stand…" (Ephesians 6:13b, NKJV). It felt like I was not doing anything;

however, He showed me I *was* doing something, I was obeying His command, *to stand.* The enemy of your soul will always try to push you out of your place: your position of prayer, faith, your heritage, purpose, family, or church. Like Jehoshaphat, you may cry out, "Here they are, rewarding us by coming to throw us out of Your possession which

> Sometimes we break strongholds in the name of Jesus, declaring God's promises, while other times we simply rest in faith.

You have given us to inherit... We do not know what to do, but our eyes are upon You" (2 Chronicles 20:11-12, NKJV). I have prayed this prayer many times! By faith we stand, believing the battle is the Lord's! God will lead you to surrender your loved one to Jesus and praise Him for the victory even while waiting (2 Chronicles 20:15-22).

Prayer combined with fasting increases our fervency and effectiveness in prayer. Fasting also sharpens our ability to hear the voice of the Spirit. Jesus said, "*When* you give... *when* you pray... *when* you fast..." (Matthew 6:2-17). He practiced this discipline and taught us to do likewise. For those committed to persevering intercessory prayer, fasting is a powerful asset to help bring breakthroughs.

At times, we are at a loss of what to pray or do not feel we can pray effectively. We may even have lost hope. In those moments, we need to be reminded of this truth: "But hope that is seen is not hope at all. Who hopes for what he already has? But if we hope for what we do not yet have, we wait for it patiently. In the same way, the Spirit helps us in our weakness. We do not know what we ought to pray for, but the Spirit himself intercedes for us with groans that words cannot express ... The Spirit intercedes for the saints in accordance with God's will" (Romans 8:24-27).

Once while praying for my niece, God showed me a vision of her on the streets, reaching out to teenage addicts. At this time in her life, she was on drugs herself. It was tearing her family apart and my sister feared for her daughter's life. Many in our family were diligently praying for her to come back to Christ. I was so moved by the hope of this vision that I sent my niece a letter, telling her what God had shown me. Joining in faith, my sister and I prayed this vision over her daughter regardless of the present reality. Jesus Himself says that there is tremendous power when two agree together in united prayer (Matthew 18:19).

This is my sister, Gonny's, story:

"Melanie suffered for a long time from the pain of rejection. My daughter wanted friends at school and because of peer pressure, she started compromising. I battled in warfare, prevailing prayer for several years laying on my face crying out to God for His grace and mercy. I pleaded based on the triumph of Jesus Christ on the cross. I knew it was a battle between 'life and death.' There were many nights when she didn't come home, and I would speak the Word of God over her life. Sometimes I would pray in the Holy Spirit all night long, battling my own fears by taking authority in Jesus' name over the demonic powers that were opposing me in my faith in God's promises for me and Melanie's future. I believed that Melanie was born with a God-given plan according to Psalm 139:16 and that none of God's purposes could be withheld from

Him according to Job 42:2. Isaiah 54:10-17 was a great comfort to me, as well, during that time. The Word of God, which cannot fail, was my hope that kept my mind, will, and emotions anchored. God's grace helped me through the storm, His love *never* failed me, and His mighty power brought me through.

> The Word of God, which cannot fail, was my hope that kept my mind, will, and emotions anchored.

"After persevering in prayer for several years, there was a breakthrough. My daughter finally brought the broken pieces of her life to Jesus and surrendered everything to Him. God has transformed her completely! He has even used all things together for good. I have been able to minister hope to so many women concerning the impossible in regard to the lives of their children and loved ones. If we have faith like a mustard seed, nothing will be impossible for us, for with God, all things are possible!"

Melanie and her husband, Phil, now serve as lead pastors for Nations Church in Los Angeles, California. She leads worship, mentors women from rough and difficult backgrounds, and has a passion to reach the people of Los Angeles. She and her husband recently started Nations Leadership Training Institute where they disciple, train, and launch people into the ministry. Many of their students are new believers and have encountered genuine transformations: former gang members and drug dealers who have a calling on their lives and are now married, in ministry, and leading their families to Christ. They also recently planted another church. To God be the glory!"

Jesus teaches us in the parable of Luke 18 that we should always pray and not give up. He tells about a widow who kept pleading before an ungodly judge to give her justice against her adversary. For some time, he refused, but finally he said to himself:

"...Even though I don't fear God or care about men, yet because this widow keeps bothering me, I will see that she gets justice, so that she won't eventually wear me out with her coming" (Luke 18:4-5).

"And the Lord said, 'Listen to what the unjust judge says. And will not God bring about justice for His chosen ones, who cry out to Him day and night? Will He keep putting them off? I tell you, He will see that they get justice, and quickly. However, when the Son of Man comes, will He find faith on the earth?'" (Luke 18:6-8).

> In prayer, we literally pry loose the hands of Satan over those we have claimed for the kingdom of God.

Just like the parable, in this life, we have an adversary who has targeted the hearts of our loved ones. In prayer, we literally pry loose the hands of Satan over those we have claimed for the kingdom of God. Prayer is like a wrecking ball beating against a seemingly unmovable wall. You may not see any change for a period of time, but suddenly the wall collapses and is overcome by the tenacious force of the ball. Jesus says, "... the violent take it (the kingdom) by force" (Matthew 11:12, NKJV). In the same way, we may not see change in our loved ones, but by faith we believe God is already doing a work on the inside.

The widow in the parable persisted with her request. Persistent prayer is counted as faith. Life can easily distract us from praying fervently. Jesus encouraged us in the kind of faith that perseveres in prayer. As we approach His coming, the Lord is asking, "When the Son of man comes, will He find faith on the earth?" (Luke 18:8). This question has always been an incentive for me to continue in faith through persevering prayer. When Jesus returns, I simply want Him to find faith in my heart. This kind of prayer ignited by the Holy Spirit Himself demonstrates the kind of faith that He is seeking. Are we calling on God with persevering faith?

When my son was struggling through his youth and got caught up in the party scene, I knew that the enemy was working to destroy his life and destiny. One day, I arrived home to find him loading his belongings to move into an apartment with a friend who was also struggling. I continued to pray for him even though I didn't see any evidence of change. I chose to declare by faith that God was working as I was encouraged to recognize this principle in scripture.

While the Israelites in Egypt were crying out to God about their yoke of slavery, Moses, their deliverer, was already on his way, sent by God to set them free (Exodus 4:20). While the women were walking toward the tomb, wondering who was going to roll the stone away so they could anoint the body of Jesus, the stone was already rolled away (Mark 16:3-4). While the church was praying fervently for Peter, who was in prison, God had already set him free and he was on his way to their prayer meeting (Acts 12:3-17). This declaration in prayer increased my faith to persevere.

One day as I was praying, God showed me a picture of Jerod teaching the Bible to young men. The heaviness of the burden in prayer was lifted and I held on to His promise though there was no visible change. Suddenly, the work of God became evident as my son chose to surrender his life completely to God and repented of his sin. The Lord has been faithful to restore his life in every area and Jerod is now thriving as a godly husband and father of three beautiful children. Jerod and his wife Tara have been serving the Lord wholeheartedly on our church staff as executive pastors. Jerod leads worship, writes powerful songs, and preaches the gospel with passion and great conviction. We know that this was a complete work of grace.

Some of you have been praying for a long time for your children or loved ones who are living without Christ. The following verses have encouraged me when I needed endurance. I also found great strength in praying these scriptures and other specific biblical truth or revelation as I received it, praying God's Word back to Him. As you read them, allow the truth of God's powerful Word to build your faith, for "faith comes by hearing, and hearing by the word of God" (Romans 10:17, NKJV).

"So do not throw away your confidence; it will be richly rewarded. You need to persevere so that when you have done the will of God, you will receive what He has promised. For in just a very little while, He who is coming will come and will not delay. But my righteous one will live by faith. And if he shrinks back, I will not be pleased with him. But we are not of those who shrink back and are destroyed, but of those who believe and are saved" (Hebrews 10:35-39).

"Keep on sowing your seed, for you never know which will grow–perhaps it all will" (Ecclesiastes 11:6, LB).

"Let us not become weary in doing good, for at the proper time we will reap a harvest if we do not give up" (Galatians 6:9).

"Those who sow in tears shall reap in joy. He who continually goes forth weeping, bearing seed for sowing, shall *doubtless* come again with rejoicing, bringing his sheaves with him" (Psalm 126:5-6, NKJV).

"All your children shall be taught by the Lord, and great shall be the peace of your children" (Isaiah 54:13, NKJV).

Andy shared his life changing story of how he came to Christ through his grandpa's prayers:

"My father died when I was twelve years old. I practically lost both parents at the same time, because my mom became an alcoholic when my father died. I felt lost and alone, not knowing who to turn to. I loved my grandfather, who had taken me to church when I was a young child. He had a great influence on my life and he always told me that he was praying for me. Unfortunately, my grandpa moved to Virginia while serving as a colonel in the Air Force. I only got to see him a couple of times per year.

Trying to find a place to belong and numbing the pain of the loss of my parents, I turned to drugs and alcohol not long after my father's death. The drugs were my escape from reality and from feeling the negativity that I didn't want to feel. As I grew up, I got into harder drugs and I believed that was all I was worth. I became a heroin addict for many years and lost all hope for my life.

At the age of twenty-five, I tried to commit suicide by taking an overdose of medication. My mom found me and rushed me to the hospital in an ambulance. Two doctors told me that I was going to die after examining me. My grandpa called me several times during this fight for my life and told me he was praying for me. He repeated, 'Andy, I am praying for you and I think you should pray, too.'

"At that very moment, I realized I could no longer live life by myself, in my own strength. I needed God in my life. I did what my grandfather said. I prayed, 'God, my life is not mine, it's Yours. Do whatever you wish.' Suddenly, I felt overcome by His presence. I rolled over and saw the silhouette of Jesus. I then fell asleep for eight hours. I hadn't slept that long for many years, because as a child I was plagued by night terrors, and as I got older, I struggled with insomnia.

While I was sleeping, the nurse took my blood. When I woke up the next morning, the doctor exclaimed, 'I do not have an explanation for this, but you are getting better!' I knew Jesus had healed me and I knew that I was going to be okay. I had hope for the first time. I was healed completely and miraculously, set free from heroin and alcohol. I went for six months to a rescue mission and did Bible studies. A friend invited me to the Live Free ministry at Calvary's Love Church and the leaders treated me like their best friend. God answered my grandpa's prayer above and beyond his expectation.

I have been transformed by Jesus Christ and, if that wasn't enough, by God's grace I served on the leadership team for our Live Free ministry for several years and loved ministering with the children in our church. God used me to minister to men and women who were struggling with addictions to bring them to Christ. I can't wait to see all God has in store. I would have died without Christ had it not been for my grandpa's persevering prayer!"

Are you praying in faith for a loved one? Do not give up praying, for God is *mighty to save!* You are powerless in your own strength to reclaim them, but your Lord is Almighty! Rise up from your discouragement and the ashes of your defeat and lay hold of His promise: "The Lord your God is with you, He is mighty to save!" (Zephaniah 3:17a).

I was lying flat on my back in a dark room fighting intense headaches. It was the day of a large community outreach with our church. A few years ago, we approached the town council and offered to provide a Kid's Zone filled with free activities for children at the annual strawberry festival. They were delighted and gladly accepted our proposal. It helped us connect with hundreds of people from our community, serve them, and show God's love. We also were able to hand out a gift packet to every family attending the Kid's Zone with the Book of Hope for children and information about our church. I was incredibly thankful for an amazing team that was prepared to connect with the families at the event and serve them, but, of course, I wanted to join them more than anything!

I had been sick all week with a high fever, which was followed by migraines. We had been praying and believing God for healing. It was 2:50 p.m. and as I was laying on my bed, I was thinking, "I'm so done with this." I turned my thought into a prayer "Lord, I'm so done. I'm done with my virus, done with my headaches. I'm done! In the name of Jesus, Satan, you are done." I got out of bed and raised my voice. "You are done." I named a few more things I had prayed for that week. Jesus Christ Himself said the words, "IT IS DONE (finished)" on the cross! I continued to declare, "I am done, Satan, in Jesus' name, you are done, and Jesus says, 'It is done.'

Christ's work on the cross is done and complete!" Immediately, a weight lifted from me and I felt much better. When my husband asked how I was doing, I responded, "God has given me the word 'done' and I'm feeling much better." Though this is not a prayer I pray in every hard situation, in this instance God was leading me this way. Suddenly the phone rang. It was my son Jerod calling to see how I was feeling.

I told him the whole story of how God was healing me by declaring the words, "It is done." He paused for a minute and then responded, "Mom, do you know what song I am recording this week?" (He was scheduled to record his first album.) "Mom, I'm recording the song 'IT IS DONE!'" Now it was my turn to be surprised. Of course, I knew that one of the worship songs he wrote is called, "It is done," but while receiving these words from God, I did not think of this song, nor did I know that he was recording that very song. God's timing, as always, was perfect, as He was confirming His Word through this encounter.

Where are you today? Are you *down* or *done?* Persevering prayer includes rising up in faith, declaring who God is and what He had done and who you are in Christ! Before you finish reading this chapter, I would encourage you to put the book down and listen to this powerful song which is available on all digital platforms.[7]

Willy Maasbach

The following interview is with my mom, Willy Maasbach, whom I love and admire as a great woman of prayer. While growing up, she planted a seed of persevering prayer in my heart. My mom lives in The Hague, The Netherlands where she and my dad pioneered a world-wide missions work and planted many churches.

Esther Terry: How did you become a woman of prayer?

Willy Maasbach: God called me into the ministry as a young woman, but I did not have anyone's support. This caused me to seek God for His help, leading, and wisdom so that He could show me the way to go. I felt completely dependent on the Lord. After I married my husband, who was an evangelist, we had a large family of eight children. My husband was often on the mission field all over the world. That left me alone and this caused me to feel an even greater dependency on the Lord. I believed the Word of God that says, "Casting all your care on Him, for He cares for you" (1 Peter 5:7, NKJV). I definitely did this, many times. I have experienced that my prayers were not in vain and that His Word was confirmed to me. Now that I am a widow, I still feel the most important task for me is to spend my time in prayer for my children and grandchildren, the church, the ministry, and the great needs in the world. I am thankful that the Bible says that we will still bear fruit in our old age and remain fresh and green (Psalm 92:14). I hope to complete this ministry of prayer until the very end.

ET: God has blessed you with eight children, twenty grandchildren, and twenty great-grandchildren who all follow Jesus. Has it always been this way?

WM: Some of my children struggled, especially during their teenage years, before they surrendered their lives completely to the Lord. As a mother, I often poured my heart out, shedding tears before the Lord during this time in their lives. I carried this need and battle for my children in prayer. I think it moved the hand of God to do His own work in their lives. God drew them to Himself and eventually they learned to know God's grace for themselves. Of course, the enemy is always trying to pull young people in another direction so that they do not surrender their lives to Jesus. Yet I have seen that we are more than conquerors through Jesus Christ. Faith is essential in order to persevere and stand on the promises of His Word that He will fulfill His purposes, also in our children.

ET: Was there anything in particular that helped you during those difficult times?

WM: With complete confidence I can say, the Word of God. The Bible says, "If you remain in me and my words remain in you, ask whatever you wish, and it will be given you" (John 15:7). His

Word will last forever. God does what He says. It helped me tremendously to trust His promises, knowing and believing that He will do what He has promised. Whatever the circumstances may be, God will work all things together for the good of those who love Him (Romans 8:28). This encouraged me to keep my focus on Jesus, who is the author and finisher of our faith.

ET: Did discouragement ever make you feel like giving up?

WM: There was a moment when I was tremendously busy with the children. I was doing an enormous load of laundry without a washing machine or dryer. It was hot outside and I saw my neighbor lying down on a lawn chair in her yard. She was reading a book and drinking lemonade. A negative feeling came over me and I thought, "What about *my* life? Is this what it is all about, constantly carrying all these heavy burdens and cares?" I cried out to God, "Please comfort and strengthen me!" Immediately, He responded, "Willy, be happy and rejoice. I will bless you because I will use your children in My service." God told me to train my children in prayer and the Word of God. He also encouraged me at that very moment saying, "I will fill you with My joy." Right then, the Holy Spirit came over me and I began laughing out loud in victory. I lifted my hands up and started to praise the Lord and the spirit of depression was broken and completely gone.

ET: What gave you the breakthrough in praying for your children?

WM: Without a doubt, it was persevering prayer in faith instead of looking at my circumstances. I learned to look at the Lord, the Almighty God, with whom all things are possible and whose name is Wonderful. Because the Scripture says, "No eye has seen, no ear has heard, no mind has conceived what God has prepared for those who love Him" (1 Corinthians 2:9). The Lord has confirmed His Word in my life, allowing me to experience many breakthroughs, miracles, signs, and wonders.

ET: Can you share about a specific miracle that happened?

WM: God Himself has worked in each of my children's and grandchildren's lives to bring them to the place He had for them. There was a particular time God placed a heavy burden in my heart to pray and fast for my son, Robert. I felt there was a battle raging against his life and his calling. He was not serving the Lord.

In prayer, God gave me a breakthrough and overwhelming victory. Exactly one week later, our phone rang, and we were told that my son had been in a car accident and had broken his neck. The doctor said it was a miracle he was still alive. The bones stayed in place, but had he moved, he would have been paralyzed or died. Though the news was devastating, by the grace of God, the Lord filled my heart with a supernatural peace. The same morning of the accident, God gave me a song, and as I sang it, God's powerful anointing and presence came over me. I did not know how the Lord would bring a change in his heart, but I knew He would.

While in the hospital, my son had an encounter with God. This was Robert's account of the event: "Jesus came to me and asked me, 'Robert, what have you done for Me in your life?' I could not answer Him, as I had never fully surrendered my life to Him. Then my father came into my room and said, 'Don't you think it is the grace of God you are not dead?' I began to weep with gratitude. He said, 'Let's pray and go home.' This is what he prayed: "Thank You, Jesus, that You are always with us and that by Your stripes, Robert is healed.' Jesus healed me at that moment and only a few days later, I walked out of the hospital. My father said something I never forgot: 'Robert, now you know your life is not your own.' Because of this, my two life scriptures are Galatians 2:20 and Acts 26:18.''

God supernaturally healed Robert and he has never been the same again. He answered God's call on his life. Robert and his wife, Virginia, and family lead Life Church in Folkstone, England. To God be the glory!

ET: What would you like to say to someone who has a child or loved one who is not serving the Lord?

WM: It is important to persevere in prayer and faith. Of course, it is always essential to build a relationship with our children through love and communication. There may also be a time to make things right and offer or ask for forgiveness. As you do these things, do not give up in prayer.

I think of the story of the mother who came to Jesus desperate for Him to deliver her daughter. She just did not give up and her daughter was set free by the power of Jesus (Matthew 15:21-28). That is why I encourage you to persevere in calling on the Lord in prayer, pleading for mercy, which we have received through Jesus Christ. I also recommend that you declare the Word of God out loud, holding fast to His promises with unwavering faith, whatever the circumstances might be. God who is faithful will also do it!

I am thankful for my mother's example. I have seen many answers to prayer in my own life and family. It has been my desire to pass on the power of persevering prayer to my own children, grandchildren, and this generation. I have been encouraged by the many examples in God's Word and, above all, by Jesus Himself who persevered fervently in prayer for the souls of mankind. One day, Jesus will receive the reward of His intercession and sacrifice when the nations of every tribe and tongue gather before His throne to worship Him.

"After this I looked and there before me was a great multitude that no one could count, from every nation, tribe, people, and language, standing before the throne and in front of the Lamb. They were wearing white robes and were holding palm branches in their hands. And they cried out in a loud voice: 'Salvation belongs to our God, who sits on the throne, and to the Lamb.' All the angels were standing around the throne and around the elders and the four living creatures. They fell down on their face before the throne and worshiped God, saying: 'Amen! Praise and glory and wisdom and thanks and honor and power and strength be to our God for ever and ever, Amen!'" (Revelation 7:9-12).

God the Father is calling us to participate with Him in preparing the reward of His inheritance that He has promised His Son. There is no greater joy!

Though I have seen many answers to prayer, there are relatives, friends, neighbors, communities and nations who have not yet opened the door of their hearts to Jesus.

Let's not give up but keep praying for those who are living without Jesus no matter how long it takes! Let's ask God to help us do what we must do and believe Him to do what we cannot do!

One of my favorite scriptures is found in Revelation 3:20: "Here I am! I stand at the door and knock. If anyone hears my voice and opens the door, I will come in and eat with him, and he with me." This speaks about God's desire for relationship with us, but it also provides us an illustration about living on mission with God. We join Him in knocking, though sometimes we may get weary of knocking and our knuckles might even get bruised in the process.

Yet we persevere in knocking along with Him, compelled by the Spirit, encouraged by His presence, believing that many will open their hearts' door and let Him in. May they experience His presence and peace through relationship with the One who gave His life for all!

> We persevere in knocking along with Him, compelled by the Spirit, encouraged by His presence, believing that many will open their hearts' door and let Him in.

"I have found there are three stages in every great work of God. First it is impossible, then it is difficult, then it is done" (Hudson Taylor).

"Not by might, nor by power, but by my Spirit, says the Lord Almighty" (Zechariah 4:6).

REFLECTION AND APPLICATION

1. What speaks to you from the Parable of the Persistent Widow (Luke 18:1-8)?

2. What does persevering prayer look like to you?

3. If waiting is never wasting, how might God use a season of delay? Have you ever experienced a delay in prayer that was later fulfilled? What did you learn through the delay?

4. Declaring God's promises, standing in faith, worshipping, and fasting are some strategies we can use while persevering in prayer. Briefly describe what each of these might look like to walk out in a practical way.

5. Is there someone you've been praying for, for some time? How has this teaching inspired your faith to continue in persistent prayer on their behalf?

6. Read Hebrews 10:35-39, Galatians 6:9, and Psalm 126:5-6. In what way do these verses strengthen and encourage you in your faith? How can you use these verses to pray God's Word back to Him? Is there another verse or story from the Bible that God has shown you during a time of delay?

7. What steps will you take this week to persevere in prayer?

ENDNOTES

1 From: *The Joy of Sharing Jesus* written by Bill Bright, 2005-2018 The Bright Media Foundation and Campus Crusade for Christ, Inc. All rights reserved. Included by permission.

2 This term is in reference to *Response Evangelism* by Randy Hurst

3 *Experiencing God Day-by-Day* by Henry & Richard Blackaby

4 *A Spirit-Empowered Church* by Alton Garrison

5 Archive Johan Maasbach World Mission, The Hague, Holland.

6 AGWM Africa, *Live/Dead Journal* (Salubris, 2012), page 162, 164. Used by permission.

7 *It is Done* by Calvary's Love